1 2 3 4 5 6 7 8 9 0 AAP 0 9 8 7 6 5

ISBN 0-87051-611-6

Accounting Trends & Techniques — Not-for-Profit Organizations

Financial Statement Reporting and Disclosure Practices

Written by
Richard F. Larkin, CPA

Updated and Revised by
Allen L. Fetterman, CPA

Edited by
Lori A. West, CPA
Technical Manager
Accounting and Auditing Publications

8841-341

PREFACE

This publication provides illustrative financial statements and related disclosures for nongovernmental not-for-profit organizations, other than health care providers. The examples contained herein have been adapted from actual examples of audited financial statements of not-for-profit organizations whose names and other identifying information have been changed. This publication is published by the Accounting and Auditing Publications team of the American Institute of Certified Public Accountants and is intended to provide practitioners with nonauthoritative practical guidance on such financial statements and disclosures.

This publication is organized to be used as a reference tool for presentations and disclosures for not-for-profit organizations as follows:

Sample financial statements are presented in the following chapters:

- Chapter 1—"Sample Statements of Financial Position"
- Chapter 2—"Sample Statements of Activity, Including Changes in Net Assets"
- Chapter 3—"Sample Statements of Cash Flows"
- Chapter 4—"Sample Statements of Functional Expenses"

Sample note disclosures are presented in the following chapters:

- Chapter 5—"Sample Disclosures—General"
- Chapter 6—"Sample Disclosures Related Primarily to the Statement of Financial Position"
- Chapter 7—"Sample Disclosures Related Primarily to the Statement of Activity and Related Statements"

Additional information is presented in the following sections:

- Chapter 8—"Financial Statements Prepared on a Basis Other Than GAAP"
- Chapter 9—"Information Outside the Financial Statements"
- Appendixes A through E (excerpts from relevant accounting literature)

The focus of this publication and the way it has been presented have been shaped by the author, others in the industry, and the AICPA staff, recognizing the need for presentation and disclosure guidance in the area of not-for-profit organizations. This publication is not a substitute for the authoritative professional pronouncements. Users of this publication are urged to refer directly to the applicable authoritative pronouncements for further guidance.

The author wishes to thank those who provided examples of financial statements, and also Susan Budak, Gregory Capin, Stanley Corfman, Margot Faivush, Julie Floch, Susan Frohlich, Larry Goldstein, J. Mark Jenkins, John Schlitt, and Joel Tanenbaum, for reviewing drafts of this publication and giving many helpful suggestions for improving it.

March 2005

TABLE OF CONTENTS

INTRODUCTION

The examples contained herein have been adapted from actual examples of audited financial statements of not-for-profit organizations whose names and other identifying information have been changed. The organization names used in this publication are fictitious. Any resemblance or similarities to real organizations is entirely coincidental and beyond the intent of the author, the staff, or the AICPA. Many of these examples as printed here omit $(000) or $(000,000) from the original; this is not noted. Accordingly, some columns and rows of numbers may not appear to add to the totals given; this is due to rounding. All years have been changed to reflect the current year as 20X2 (with 20X1 as the prior year and 20X3 as the succeeding year).

This publication was originally issued in 1999 as a Practice Aid titled *Financial Statement Presentation and Disclosure Practices for Not-for-Profit Organizations.* This version of the document has been renamed *Accounting Trends & Techniques—Not-for-Profit Organizations,* and has been updated to encompass material related to standards issued or effective through March 1, 2005, including Financial Accounting Standards Board (FASB) Statement of Financial Accounting Standards No. 133, *Accounting for Derivative Instruments and Hedging Activities,* on derivatives, and FASB Statement No. 136, *Transfers of Assets to a Not-for-Profit Organization or Charitable Trust That Raises or Holds Contributions for Others,* on pass-through gifts. Most other recent standards either would not normally require any change in reporting practices specific to not-for-profits, or are not applicable to them. Also included is some material on the Sarbanes-Oxley Act.

Some examples refer to "The University" or some other specific type of not-for-profit organization. This merely reflects the fact that certain types of transactions and balances are found especially often in the type of organization named. It is not intended to imply that other types of organizations cannot use similar presentations and disclosures if appropriate, or that organizations of the named type must use any particular format.

Requirements for the use of specific titles and, for the most part, formats of financial statements of not-for-profit organizations are not set forth in the professional literature (for example, in FASB Statement No. 117, *Financial Statements of Not-for-Profit Organizations,* FASB always refers to, "A statement of...," not, "The Statement of...," and in paragraph 83 uses the terminology, "...statement of financial position (balance sheet)..." to indicate that no particular term is being mandated). The example titles in this publication are not intended to indicate that these are the only acceptable titles. (See also footnote 2 to Chapter 3 of the AICPA Audit and Accounting Guide *Not-for-Profit Organizations* [the Guide].[*]) Also, the choice of a particular format (for example,

---

[*] References throughout this publication to the AICPA Audit and Accounting Guide *Not-for-Profit Organizations* are to the edition with conforming changes as of May 1, 2004.

multicolumnar) for one statement does not limit the choices available for other statements, so long as all required information is presented.

Paragraph 69 of FASB Statement No. 117 encourages, but does not require, the presentation of prior-year comparative financial information. Some of the examples in this publication include comparative information; in the interests of space, not all do so. Some organizations which present information in a multicolumnar format choose to present only a total column in some or all statements for the prior period. If this is done, paragraphs 3.20 and 3.21 of the Guide should be consulted for guidance.

Many organizations follow the practice of including one of the standard phrases, "The accompanying notes are an integral part of the financial statements," or "See accompanying notes," or variations thereof, at the bottom of each financial statement. Others insert references to specific notes near the captions, or parts of other notes, to which the notes refer. Neither practice is illustrated here; organizations should follow their own preferences in this regard.

Note that information in the disclosure examples in Chapters 6 and 7 often is related to both financial position and activity statements, so both chapters should be consulted for examples on various subjects.

For example, disclosures about split-interest agreements refer to both the assets and liabilities associated with such agreements, as well as the related contribution revenue. These sample disclosures are included in Chapter 7, but are also relevant to Chapter 6.

These disclosures are intended as nonauthoritative guidance only. Sample notes are not necessarily complete or unedited reproductions of the originals. In some cases, certain disclosures may be missing from the sample statements or notes because in the originals this information was provided elsewhere in the statements or notes.

For further guidance on preparation of financial statements and related disclosures specific to not-for-profit organizations, see the following:

- FASB Statement of Financial Accounting Standards No. 116, *Accounting for Contributions Received and Contributions Made*
- FASB Statement of Financial Accounting Standards No. 117, *Financial Statements of Not-for-Profit Organizations*
- FASB Statement of Financial Accounting Standards No. 124, *Accounting for Certain Investments Held by Not-for-Profit Organizations*
- FASB Statement of Financial Accounting Standards No. 136, *Transfers of Assets to a Not-for-Profit Organization or Charitable Trust That Raises or Holds Contributions for Others*
- AICPA Technical Publications
- AICPA Audit and Accounting Guide *Not-for-Profit Organizations*
- AICPA's *Checklists and Illustrative Financial Statements for Not-for-Profit Organizations*

CHAPTER 1: Sample Statements of Financial Position

Financial Accounting Standards Board (FASB) Statement of Financial Accounting Standards No. 117, *Financial Statements of Not-for-Profit Organizations*, requires the following in a statement of financial position:

- Total assets
- Total liabilities
- Net assets by class and in total
- Information about liquidity
- Reasonably homogeneous asset and liability categories

The examples in this chapter which are in a multicolumnar format show the columns labeled with either names of organizations (combining statements), or funds, but not classes of net assets. While it is not prohibited to have the columns represent the net asset classes, this is not shown because of the FASB's statement in paragraph 94 of FASB Statement No. 117, that classification of assets and liabilities by net asset class should be permitted but not required. Many believe that, because the reporting model in Statement No. 117 is based on net assets, in most cases, specific assets and liabilities are neither unrestricted nor restricted, and that any attempt to categorize them as such results in arbitrary classifications without an objective basis. Columnar formats showing funds as the columns all show the classes of net assets separately in the Net Assets section of the statement.

Accounting literature does not specify whether certain required information should be presented on the face of the statement of financial position or in the notes to the financial statements. One example is asset valuation allowances. Some organizations include them as part of the asset caption on the balance sheet; others disclose them in a note. Allowances for uncollectible receivables are more often included in the asset caption. Accumulated depreciation is more often disclosed in a note together with details of the components of fixed assets. Other examples are information about the nature and amount of restrictions on net assets and the composition of the investment portfolio. Some organizations present this information on the face of the balance sheet, while other organizations include this information in the notes.

COLUMNAR FORMATS

The following is an example of a single-column statement for a large institution. This statement includes a liability representing amounts held by the university under agency agreements with other organizations such as on-campus student organizations. The related assets are included in their appropriate categories—cash, and others. In a balance sheet disaggregated by fund or net asset class, these assets and related liabilities would be included in the unrestricted section.

Because these assets and the transactions affecting them do not belong to the reporting university, no amounts related thereto would be included in the university's statement of activities. However, a statement of cash flows prepared using the direct method would include related cash receipts and disbursements as operating cash flows (per AICPA Audit and Accounting Guide *Not-for-Profit Organizations* [the Guide], paragraph 3.16). (Also see the FGH University example in Chapter 3 of this publication.) A statement of cash flows prepared using the indirect method would not show any caption for these because they will always net out against the change in the balance sheet liability.

FGH University
Statement of Financial Position
at July 31, 20X2 and 20X1

	20X2	20X1
Assets:		
Cash and cash equivalents	$316,388	$159,041
Accounts receivable, net of allowances of $7,439 and $4,236	102,339	91,827
Inventories and prepaid expenses	53,856	48,907
Contributions receivable, net of allowances of $18,600 and $18,000	114,618	135,407
Student loans receivable, net of allowances of $5,230 and $5,190	65,267	61,555
Other loans receivable (principally faculty mortgages)	73,067	68,805
Investments at market	5,031,550	4,338,480
Net assets of [*Affiliated Organization*]	319,471	280,057
Plant facilities, net of accumulated depreciation	1,124,259	1,058,354
Collections of works of art (Note X)	—	—
Total assets	$7,200,815	$6,242,433
Liabilities and net assets:		
Liabilities:		
Accounts payable and accrued expenses	$335,416	$270,385
Collateral for security lending agreements	125,423	91,231
Income beneficiary share of living trust investments	170,029	143,940
Notes and bonds payable	688,149	624,361
Agency funds held for others	41,322	36,811
U.S. Government refundable loan funds	42,768	40,668
Commitments and contingencies	—	—
Total liabilities	1,403,107	1,207,396

	20X2	20X1
Net assets:		
Unrestricted:		
Designated for operations	722,129	611,356
Investment in plant facilities	660,481	646,798
Endowment gains and funds functioning as endowment	2,449,836	2,010,137
[*Affiliated Organization*]	319,471	280,057
Total unrestricted	4,151,917	3,548,348
Temporarily restricted	306,550	259,047
Permanently restricted	1,339,241	1,227,642
Total net assets	5,797,708	5,035,037
Total liabilities and net assets	$7,200,815	$6,242,433

FGH University has presented in the balance sheet details regarding the components of the unrestricted class of net assets. This is not required to be disclosed. However, total unrestricted net assets is a required disclosure. Alternatively, the components of unrestricted net assets could be presented in the notes to the financial statements.

FGH University has presented a line on the balance sheet for commitments and contingencies. Some organizations choose not to present such a line on the balance sheet. It is not required.

· ·

The following example illustrates combining financial statements for two affiliated organizations.

The BCD Foundation
Combining Balance Sheet
December 31, 20X2

	The BCD Foundation	The [Affiliated] Foundation	Total
Assets:			
Cash and cash equivalents	$ 4,364,031		$ 4,364,031
Program-related loans receivable	371,729		371,729
Investments, at market	115,747,252	$2,873,174	118,620,426
Contributions receivable from charitable remainder trusts	5,734,337		5,734,337
Beneficial interest in:			
Unitrust agreement	1,409,932		1,409,932
Perpetual trusts	2,405,695		2,405,695
Other assets	164,661		164,661
Total assets	$130,197,637	$2,873,174	$133,070,811

(*continued*)

	The BCD Foundation	The [Affiliated] Foundation	Total
Liabilities and Net Assets:			
Accounts payable and accrued expenses	$ 28,385		$ 28,385
Grants payable	540,222	$ 270,711	810,933
Liability under unitrust agreement	715,482		715,482
Commitment	—		—
Total liabilities	1,284,089	270,711	1,554,800
Net assets:			
Unrestricted:			
Donor advised	48,618,267		48,618,267
Field-of-interest	14,348,619	2,602,463	16,951,082
Designated	5,124,057		5,124,057
Discretionary	51,988,122		51,988,122
Total unrestricted	120,079,065	2,602,463	122,681,528
Temporarily restricted	1,754,215		1,754,215
Permanently restricted	7,080,268		7,080,268
Total net assets	128,913,548	2,602,463	131,516,011
Total liabilities and net assets	$130,197,637	$2,873,174	$133,070,811

The following is an example of a statement presented in the "assets, less liabilities, equals net assets" format. This is especially appropriate when liabilities are relatively small compared to assets, but can be used by any organization.

LMN Museum
Statement of Financial Position
June 30, 20X2

ASSETS	
Cash	$ 480,241
Grants and contributions receivable	86,488
Prepaid expenses	1,761,606
Inventories	856,817
Notes receivable	28,515
Long-term investments:	
Pooled investments	107,754,307
Beneficial interests in trusts and insurance	2,789,580
Real estate and oil leases	1,116,665
Fixed assets:	
Grounds and buildings, net	11,247,907
Equipment and vehicles, net	2,268,665
Library, art, and garden collections carried at no value (Note X)	0
Total assets	128,624,501

Less: LIABILITIES	
Accounts payable and accrued expenses	1,318,882
Obligations under unitrust and annuity agreements	1,326,104
Notes payable	35,340
Commitments and contingencies	0
Total liabilities	2,680,326
NET ASSETS	
Unrestricted—	
Available for operations	675,165
Designated for special projects	376,650
Invested in fixed assets	13,173,739
Board-designated endowment	43,495,253
Total unrestricted	57,720,807
Temporarily restricted—	
Specific purpose funds	3,074,154
Beneficial interests in trusts and insurance	1,146,281
Term endowment	20,438,253
Total temporarily restricted	24,658,688
Permanently restricted—	
Beneficial interests in trust and insurance	400,000
Endowment	43,164,680
Total permanently restricted	43,564,680
Total net assets	$125,944,175

The information regarding the components of unrestricted, temporarily restricted, and permanently restricted net assets could be presented in the notes to the financial statements.

The following example uses the columnar format by fund. Note that the net assets section includes amounts in the appropriate columns. For some organizations, this format may better track the way finances are managed internally. This financial statement is also illustrated in the next example, using a different presentation.

AIC Association
Balance Sheet
December 31, 20X2 and 20X1

	20X2			20X1		
	Operating Fund	*Endowment Fund*	*Total*	*Operating Fund*	*Endowment Fund*	*Total*
Assets:						
Cash	$ 2,732	$ 685	$ 3,417	$ 2,284	$ 558	$ 2,842
Investments	18,312	12,246	30,558	16,109	10,869	26,978

(continued)

	20X2			20X1		
	Operating Fund	*Endowment Fund*	*Total*	*Operating Fund*	*Endowment Fund*	*Total*
Accounts receivable	6,315		6,315	5,205		5,205
Inventories	3,677		3,677	2,336		2,336
Prepaid expenses	2,320		2,320	1,762		1,762
Property and equipment	4,450		4,450	4,193		4,193
Total assets	$37,806	$ 12,931	$50,737	$31,889	$ 11,427	$43,316
Liabilities and net assets:						
Accounts payable	$ 6,792		$ 6,792	$ 5,362		$ 5,362
Accrued expenses	755		755	560		560
Deferred member dues	5,045		5,045	7,308		7,308
Unearned subscriptions	6,392		6,392	3,625		3,625
Total liabilities	18,984		18,984	16,855		16,855
Net assets:						
Unrestricted	15,233	$ 2,412	17,645	13,253	$ 2,003	15,256
Temporarily restricted	3,589	—	3,589	1,781	—	1,781
Permanently restricted	—	10,519	10,519	—	9,424	9,424
Total net assets	18,822	12,931	31,753	15,034	11,427	26,461
Total liabilities and net assets	$37,806	$12,931	$50,737	$31,889	$11,427	$43,316

LAYERED FORMATS

Prior to the issuance of FASB Statement No. 117, this format was more popular. The last section of this statement, showing grand totals of assets, liabilities, and net assets, now required by FASB Statement No. 117, was not necessarily included. When there are numerous funds presented separately, this format makes it easier to include complete comparative information by fund or class in a more compact arrangement than does the columnar format. This is also referred to as a "pancake" format. Note that this is the same financial statement as the previous example.

AIC Association
Balance Sheet
December 31, 20X2 and 20X1

Operating Fund						
	20X2	*20X1*			*20X2*	*20X1*
Assets:			Liabilities and net assets:			
Cash	$ 2,732	$ 2,284	Accounts payable		$ 6,792	$ 5,362
Investments	18,312	16,109	Accrued expenses		755	560
Accounts receivable	6,315	5,205	Deferred member dues		5,045	7,308
Inventories	3,677	2,336	Unearned subscriptions		6,392	3,625
Prepaid expenses	2,320	1,762	Total liabilities		18,984	16,855

	20X2	20X1		20X2	20X1
Property and equipment	4,450	4,193	Net assets:		
			Unrestricted	15,233	13,253
			Temporarily restricted	3,589	1,781
			Total net assets	18,822	15,034
Total assets	$37,806	$31,889	Total liabilities and net assets	$37,806	$31,889
Endowment Fund					
Assets:			Net assets:		
Cash	$ 685	$ 558	Unrestricted	$ 2,412	$ 2,003
Investments	12,246	10,869	Permanently restricted	10,519	9,424
Total assets	$12,931	$11,427	Total net assets	$12,931	$11,427
Total All Funds					
			Total liabilities	$18,984	$16,855
			Net assets		
			Unrestricted	17,645	15,256
			Temporarily restricted	3,589	1,781
			Permanently restricted	10,519	9,424
			Total net assets	31,753	26,461
Total assets	$50,737	$43,316	Total liabilities and net assets	$50,737	$43,316

The following statement illustrates a classified balance sheet format, where the traditional method of showing liquidity-presenting current assets and liabilities separately with subtotals of each is used. Other methods of showing liquidity are discussed in FASB Statement No. 117, paragraph 12, and are illustrated in the other examples in this chapter, and in some of the footnotes in Chapter 6. Note that breaking out the building fund (calculated as net fixed assets less the mortgage) from total net assets reveals that this club actually has a deficit in its general fund, even though it has a working capital surplus.

LKJ Club
Balance Sheet
June 30, 20X2 and 20X1

	Assets			Liabilities and Net Assets	
	20X2	20X1		20X2	20X1
Current assets:			Current liabilities:		
Cash	$ 157	$ 123	Current portion of mortgage	$ 44	$ 58
Accounts receivable	475	480			
Inventories, at lower of cost or market	101	99	Accounts payable	153	142
Prepaid expenses	55	48	Accrued salaries, taxes and expense	184	165

(*continued*)

	Assets			Liabilities and Net Assets	
	20X2	20X1		20X2	20X1
Total current assets	788	750	Accrued vacation	26	21
Deferred compensation investments	498	433	Unearned dues	344	342
			Total current liabilities	751	728
Land, building, and equipment:					
Land	2,063	2,063			
Building	2,491	2,305	Deferred compensation	495	419
Club house furniture and equipment	756	736	Building mortgage	307	365
Kitchen equipment	190	187	Other long-term debt	450	569
Office equipment	77	76	Total liabilities	2,003	2,081
China, linen, and silverware	15	15			
	5,592	5,382	Net assets—unrestricted:		
			General fund	(366)	(475)
			Building fund	2,835	2,661
Less: accumulated depreciation	(2,406)	(2,298)	Total net assets	2,469	2,186
	3,186	3,084			
Total assets	$4,472	$4,267	Total liabilities and net assets	$4,472	$4,267

If the club in the preceding balance sheet issues stock to its members, representing equity interests in the club, FASB Statement No. 150, *Accounting for Certain Financial Instruments with Characteristics of both Liabilities and Equity,* requires the entity to disclose the potential liability to redeem the equity shares. Examples of disclosures are in Chapter 6 of this publication.

SELECTED SECTIONS OF THE STATEMENT

The following example illustrates the net assets section of a balance sheet showing net assets both summarized by class and in detail by fund or other internal grouping. This detail can also be presented in a note; see examples in Chapter 6. Note the 20X1 data is not a complete presentation under generally accepted accounting principles (GAAP); see the Guide, paragraph 3.20.

STG Organization
Statement of Financial Position [Net assets section]
June 30, 20X2, with comparative totals as of June 30, 20X1

	20X2	20X1
Net assets:		
Unrestricted	$ 448,339	$387,838
Temporarily restricted	397,689	387,810

	20X2	20X1
Permanently restricted	192,871	176,724
Total net assets	$ 1,038,899	$952,372

	20X2				20X1
	Unrestricted	*Temporarily Restricted*	*Permanently Restricted*	*Total*	*Total*
Detail of net assets:					
Accumulated deficit from operations	$ (9,481)			$ (9,481)	$(11,718)
Donor-restricted or Museum-designated for future purposes	18,579	$ 37,725	$3,700	60,004	60,618
Funding for property, improvements, and equipment	8,979	211,393		220,372	221,351
Funding for acquisitions	275	20,318		20,593	20,735
Donor-restricted endowment and Board-designated assets functioning as endowment	429,987	128,253	189,171	747,411	661,386
Total net assets	$448,339	$397,689	$192,871	$1,038,899	$952,372

Many clubs issue capital stock to their members; therefore the format of the equity section of their balance sheets often looks similar to that of a commercial business.

	20X2	20X1
Members' equity:		
Capital stock—$500 par value; 65 and 65 shares authorized and 65 and 64 issued at December 31, 20X2 and 20X1, respectively	32,500	32,000
Retained earnings	738,667	744,223
Total members' equity (unrestricted)	771,167	776,223

•••••••••••••••••••••••

Some clubs consider members' initiation fees as equivalent to paid-in capital, and report it separately from accumulated operating results, as follows.

Members' equity:	
Initiation fees	$ 180,000
Retained (deficit)	(11,000)
Total members' equity (unrestricted)	$ 169,000

CHAPTER 2: Sample Statements of Activity, Including Changes in Net Assets

Financial Accounting Standards Board (FASB) Statement of Financial Accounting Standards No. 117, *Financial Statements of Not-for-Profit Organizations*, is not specific as to permissible methods of presenting the information required in a statement of activity. It requires presentation of the following for the entity as a whole:

- Change in net assets in total and by class.
- Revenues, expenses by function, gains, losses, and reclassifications in reasonably homogeneous groups (expenses by function may be on the face of the statement of activities or in a note—see a further comment about this in Chapter 7, under "Expenses"). Note that reclassifications should always net to zero.
- Total fund-raising expenses included on the face of the statement or in the notes.
- Revenues and expenses presented gross (except investment expenses, such as management or advisory fees, which may be netted if the amount is disclosed).

While a formal reconciliation of net assets from the beginning of the year to the end of the year is not technically required by professional literature, it is often presented, either as part of the statement of activities or as a separate statement.

FASB Statement No. 117 does not define a measure of operations, but permits organizations wide latitude in choosing how to present the sequence of revenues, expenses, gains, and losses, so long as any measure of operations is in a statement which includes at least the total change in unrestricted net assets. See also the sample notes on this subject in Chapter 7 of this publication. Also, a note must describe the nature of the reported measure of operations or the items excluded from operations if the organization's use of the term "operations" is unclear from the face of the statement.

Accordingly, practice is very diverse for this statement, especially as to the sequence of items. The following examples reflect this diversity by illustrating the following presentations:

- One column versus four columns
  — Presentation of the unrestricted class in more than one column
- Presentation of combining statements for affiliated entities
- Presentation of a measure of operations
- Presentation of expenses above revenue
- Regarding investment return:
  — All investment return in operations
  — All investment return outside of operations

— Interest, dividend, and other investment income in operations, capital gains outside operations

— Interest, dividends, and realized gains in operations, unrealized gains outside operations

— Endowment earnings up to a set spending rate in operations, all other components of return outside operations

• Regarding private foundations and other grant-making organizations:
  — Presentation of grants awarded as a deduction from investment income versus with other expenses

  — Presentation of federal excise tax as a deduction from investment income versus with other expenses

COLUMNAR ARRANGEMENTS

The following example illustrates a multicolumn format by class, with an intermediate measure of operations. Other matters to note are: (1) auxiliary expenses are netted against revenue, but gross amounts are presented; (2) this format makes it clear that reclassifications do not change total net assets; and (3) collection activity is reported separately (required if collections are not capitalized).

FGH Museum
Statement of Activities
For the Year Ended December 31, 20X2

	Unrestricted	Temporarily Restricted	Permanently Restricted	Total
Operating support and revenues:				
Contributions	$ 4,084,332	$21,158,039		$25,242,371
Exhibition and project support	5,318,618			5,318,618
Admissions	5,144,142			5,144,142
Auxiliary revenue	$ 8,080,174			
Auxiliary expenses, including cost of sales	(8,851,832)	(771,658)		(771,658)
Investment income	425,267	5,601		430,868
Membership income	980,235			980,235
In-kind contributions	518,587			518,587
Other	920,005			920,005
	16,619,528	21,163,640		37,783,168

	Unrestricted	Temporarily Restricted	Permanently Restricted	Total
Net assets released from restrictions:				
General support	1,698,329	(1,698,329)		
Exhibition and projects	409,531	(409,531)		
Total operating support and revenues	18,727,388	19,055,780		37,783,168
Operating expenses:				
Museum programs:				
Exhibition and projects	16,523,269			16,523,269
Curatorial and collection maintenance	5,473,938			5,473,938
Public service	1,842,632			1,842,632
Education	768,067			768,067
Total program expenses	24,607,906			24,607,906
Supporting services:				
Management and general	3,781,372			3,781,372
Fundraising	1,550,276			1,550,276
Membership	861,593			861,593
Total supporting services	6,193,241			6,193,241
Total operating expenses	30,801,147			30,801,147
Excess (deficiency) of operating support and revenues over operating expenses	(12,073,759)	19,055,780		6,982,021
Nonoperating support and revenues, expenses, gains, and losses:				
Contributions for endowment and funds functioning as endowment	278,595		$2,932,194	3,210,789
Contributions for capital construction	225,206	2,062,363		2,287,569
Contributions for art acquisition	356,250	22,500		378,750
Net realized gain on sale of investments	1,267,033	24,670	101,708	1,393,411
Net unrealized appreciation on investments	685,001	13,611	56,887	755,499
Change in net assets before other changes	(9,261,674)	21,178,924	3,090,789	15,008,039
Changes in net assets related to collection items not capitalized:				
Proceeds from sale of collection items	325,000			325,000

(continued)

	Unrestricted	Temporarily Restricted	Permanently Restricted	Total
Collection items purchased	(452,946)			(452,946)
Change in net assets	(9,389,620)	21,178,924	3,090,789	14,880,093
Net assets—beginning of year	37,245,633	12,700,745	15,885,300	65,831,678
Net assets—end of year	$27,856,013	$33,879,669	$18,976,089	$80,711,771

This statement of activity includes a description of the purpose of each expense category as part of the caption, and percentages that major categories bear to total revenue or to program and supporting expenses.

This statement reports the cost of direct donor benefits as a supporting service in the functional expense section. AICPA Technical Practice Aid 6140.08, Functional Category of the Costs of Direct Donor Benefits, provides alternative presentations. For example, the cost of direct donor benefits may be shown as a separate (deduction) line immediately following special events revenue.

This example also shows a change in accounting.

The [Disease] Association
Statement of Activities—For the Year Ended June 30, 20X2

	Unrestricted	Permanently Restricted	Temporarily Restricted	Total	Percent
Revenues, gains, and other support:					
Support from the public:					
Contributions	$104,953	$19,126	$2,120	$126,199	25
Legacies and bequests	64,445	48,731	1,314	114,490	22
Special events	102,535	3,649	—	106,184	21
Other special fund-raising activities	16,925	458	—	17,383	3
Merchandise and other in-kind contributions, at fair value	16,279	339	—	16,618	3
Contributed services, at fair value	—	4,264	—	4,264	1
Contributions raised indirectly from federated fund-raising organizations	30,480	11,077	—	41,557	9
Total support from the public	335,617	87,644	3,434	426,695	84
Grants from government agencies	—	4,103	—	4,103	1
Investment income:					
Interest and dividends, net	27,328	1,276	115	28,719	6
Realized investment gains, net	330	445	1,008	1,783	
Unrealized investment gains (losses), net	(3,472)	62	225	(3,185)	(1)
Total investment income, net	24,186	1,783	1,348	27,317	5
Income from exchange transactions	51,777	—	—	51,777	10
Other gains	672	68	—	740	
Total revenues, gains, and other support	412,252	93,598	4,782	510,632	100

	Unrestricted	Permanently Restricted	Temporarily Restricted	Total	Percent
Net assets released from restrictions:					
Satisfaction of activity restrictions	41,439	(41,439)	—	—	
Satisfaction of equipment acquisition restrictions	2,382	(2,382)	—	—	
Expiration of explicit and implicit time restrictions	21,011	(21,011)	—	—	
Total net assets released from restrictions	$ 64,832	$(64,832)	—	—	
Expenses:					
Program services:					
Research—financial support provided to academic institutions and scientists and conduct of epidemiological studies seeking new knowledge for the causes, cures, and prevention of [*disease*]	$ 93,384	$	—	93,384	22
Prevention—programs that provide the public and health professionals with information and education to prevent [*disease*] occurrence or to reduce risk of developing [*disease*]	81,698	—	—	81,698	19
Detection/treatment—programs that are directed at finding [*disease*] before it is clinically apparent and that provide information and education about [*disease*] treatments cure, recurrence, symptom management, and pain control	52,628	—	—	52,628	13
Patient services—programs to assist [*disease*] patients and their families and ease the burden of [*disease*] for them	69,066	—	—	69,066	17
Total program services	296,776	—	—	296,776	71
Supporting services:					
Management and general—direction of the overall affairs of the [*charity*] through executive, financial, and administrative services	28,109	—	—	28,109	7
Direct donor benefits—cost of benefits provided to donors at special events	16,502			16,502	
Fund-raising—programs to secure charitable financial support for programs and supporting services	69,836	—	—	69,836	21
Unallocated payments to affiliated organizations	4,663	—	—	4,663	1
Total supporting services	119,110	—	—	119,110	29
Total program and supporting services expenses	415,886	—	—	415,886	100
Expenses related to exchange transactions	56,271	—	—	56,271	
Reorganization expenses	2,660	—	—	2,660	
Total expenses	474,817	—	—	474,817	

(*continued*)

	Unrestricted	Permanently Restricted	Temporarily Restricted	Total	Percent
Change in net assets before cumulative effect of accounting change	2,267	28,766	4,782	35,815	
Cumulative effect of accounting change	4,908	18,576	12,679	36,163	
Change in net assets	7,175	47,342	17,461	71,978	
Net assets, beginning of year	446,880	84,719	27,781	559,380	
Net assets, end of year	$454,055	$132,061	$45,242	$631,358	

The following illustrates a columnar format, with the total column to the left of the captions. Note that some of the temporarily restricted net assets released from restrictions go into the operating portion of the unrestricted class and some into the "other" (nonoperating) portion.

MNO University
Statement of Activities for the Year Ended June 30, 20X2

Total			Unrestricted	Restricted Temporarily	Permanently
	Revenues and other support:				
$ 307,849	Tuition and fees, net of discounts		$307,849		
35,783	State appropriations		35,783		
304,108	Sponsored programs		304,108		
68,527	Contributions		15,703	$52,824	
86,244	Investment income		53,084	33,160	
968,446	Hospitals and physician practices		968,446		
75,180	Sales and services of auxiliary enterprises		75,180		
68,746	Other educational activities		68,746		
20,018	Independent operations		20,018		
	Net assets released from restrictions		85,047	(85,047)	
1,934,901			1,933,964	937	
	Expenses:				
	Program:				
406,754	Instruction		406,754		
238,247	Research		238,247		
936,449	Hospitals and physician practices		936,449		
84,204	Auxiliary enterprises		84,204		
65,460	Other educational activities		65,460		
21,808	Student services		21,808		
19,508	Independent operations		19,508		
	Support:				
37,318	Academic support		37,318		

Total		Unrestricted	Restricted Temporarily	Permanently
74,244	Management and general	74,244		
6,223	Fundraising	6,223		
1,890,215		1,890,215		
44,686	Increase in net assets before nonoperating revenues, net gains, reclassifications, and other	43,749	937	
	Nonoperating revenues, net gains, reclassifications, and other:			
197,185	Gain on investments, net	56,614	125,292	$15,279
57,130	Investment income	48,089	8,555	486
57,862	Contributions	29,122	8,200	20,540
1,529	Other, net	(59,537)	38,980	22,086
(107,502)	Postretirement benefit transition obligation	(107,502)		
	Net assets released from restrictions	13,288	(13,288)	
250,890	Increase in net assets	23,823	168,676	58,391
3,243,001	Net assets, beginning of year	2,078,814	464,394	699,793
$3,493,891	Net assets, end of year	$2,102,637	$633,070	$758,184

The following example illustrates a single-column format for a large, complex institution. This format makes it easier than does the multicolumn format to present comparative data. Again, note that some of the temporarily restricted net assets released from restrictions go into the operating portion of the unrestricted class, and some into the "other" (nonoperating) portion.

Note that expenses are presented by natural classification. Thus, expenses by function will be presented in the notes.

HJL University
Statement of Activities
Years Ended August 31, 20X2 and 20X1

	20X2	20X1
Unrestricted net assets activity		
Revenues:		
Student income:		
Undergraduate programs	$130,556	$123,916
Graduate programs	128,250	121,876
Room and board	50,022	47,923
Total student income	308,828	293,715
Sponsored research support (primarily federal):		
Direct costs—University	295,803	274,889
Direct costs—[*Affiliated Research Center*]	188,492	175,780

(*continued*)

	20X2	20X1
Indirect costs	93,428	87,233
Total sponsored research support	577,723	537,902
Expendable gifts in support of operations	93,169	82,634
Investment income:		
Endowment income distributed for operations	120,400	103,385
Endowment gains distributed for operations	40,940	51,596
Other investment income	59,428	57,596
Total investment income	220,768	212,577
Other income:		
Special program fees	106,480	90,923
Auxiliary activities (excluding room and board)	94,541	95,395
Other	14,175	17,869
Total other income	215,196	204,187
Total revenues	1,415,684	1,331,015
Net assets released from restrictions	17,964	11,546
Expenses:		
Salaries and benefits	491,576	475,908
Student financial aid	65,139	65,537
Depreciation	92,320	77,428
[*Affiliated Research Center*]	188,492	175,780
Auxiliary activities (including room and board)	150,600	157,420
Institutional support	227,333	211,520
Other operating expenses	135,097	118,604
Total expenses	1,350,557	1,282,197
Excess of revenues and net assets released over expenses	83,091	60,364
Other changes in unrestricted net assets:		
Expendable gifts invested in the endowment	5,112	1,930
Reinvested endowment gains	414,962	223,967
Net increase in [*Affiliated Organization*] net assets	39,414	3,349
Capital and other gifts released from restrictions	41,250	39,922
Other investment income invested in the endowment	12,084	16,662
Other additions	7,656	16,647
Net change in unrestricted net assets	603,569	362,841
Temporarily restricted net assets activity		
Gifts, and promises to give (pledges)	104,680	122,651
Temporarily restricted return from endowment investments	3,006	1,629
Living trust investment income and actuarial adjustment	(6,331)	4,599
Other investment income	5,362	1,668
Net assets released from restrictions	(17,964)	(11,546)
Reclassification of capital and other gifts released from restrictions	(41,250)	(39,922)

	20X2	20X1
Net change in temporarily restricted net assets	47,503	79,079
Permanently restricted net assets activity		
Gifts and pledges	62,838	54,499
Permanently restricted return from endowment investments	24,350	12,293
Living trust investment income and actuarial adjustment	21,958	13,842
Other investment income	2,453	601
Net change in permanently restricted net assets	111,599	81,235
Net change in total net assets	762,671	523,155
Total net assets, beginning of year	5,035,037	4,511,882
Total net assets, end of year	$5,797,708	$5,035,037

The following example illustrates use of a multicolumn statement for the unrestricted net asset class with a single column for the restricted net asset classes. The subdivision emphasizes the extent to which the surplus from Program 2 is used to subsidize other functions. Although the line items in the expense section of this statement are natural expense categories, the presence of the columns for the functions makes this statement also serve the purpose of the matrix of functional expenses required for voluntary health and welfare organizations. This format works best for organizations with a small number of programs or funds; otherwise the focus on the entity as a whole can be lost.

RST Charity
Statement of Activities
Year Ended December 31, 20X2

	Program Services		Management and General	Fundraising	20X2 Total
	Program 1	Program 2			
Changes in unrestricted net assets:					
Revenues and other support:					
Registration fees	—	$10,504,099			$10,504,099
Government contracts:					
Activity 1	$ 792,500	—	—	—	792,500
Activity 2	1,546,000	—	—	—	1,546,000
Contributions	—	115,154	—	$3,804	118,958
Interest income	—	101,295	—	—	101,295
Donated services	—	165,421	—	—	165,421
	2,338,500	10,885,969	—	3,804	13,228,273
Net assets released from restrictions:					
Satisfaction of program restrictions	—	60,485	—	—	60,485
Total unrestricted revenues	2,338,500	10,946,454	—	3,804	13,288,758

(*continued*)

| | Program Services | | Management | | 20X2 |
	Program 1	Program 2	and General	Fundraising	Total
Expenses:					
Salaries	3,600,651	906,809	701,160	25,347	5,233,967
Employment benefits and payroll taxes	969,465	244,624	188,955	9,885	1,412,929
Temporary help	—	26,084	22,489	—	48,573
Meetings and travel	607,718	764,283	52,987	1,762	1,426,750
Subcontractors	514,840	—	—		514,840
Professional education programs and projects	14,459	75,050	58,018	—	147,527
Other purchased services	373,398	690,375	333,888	—	1,397,661
Telephone, telecommunications, and utilities	346,336	10,158	7,853	—	364,347
Publications	82,043	—	—	—	82,043
Equipment leases	32,047	573	443	—	33,063
Repairs and maintenance	66,513	90,591	70,032	—	227,136
Rent	434,753	18,051	13,954	—	466,758
Postage	92,145	9,122	7,052	—	108,319
Depreciation and amortization	428,479	18,137	14,020	—	460,636
Donated services	—	165,421	—	—	165,421
Other	182,852	105,164	77,408	6,342	371,766
Total expenses	7,745,699	3,124,442	1,548,259	43,336	12,461,736
(Decrease) increase in unrestricted net assets	$(5,407,199)	$7,822,012	$(1,548,259)	$(39,532)	827,022
Change in temporarily restricted net assets:					
Contributions					112,196
Net assets released from restrictions					(60,485)
Increase in temporarily restricted net assets					51,711
Increase in net assets					878,733
Net assets, beginning of year					3,113,639
Net assets, end of year					$ 3,992,372

The following illustrates a multicolumn statement with unrestricted net asset class subdivided into the traditional funds. This format also works best for organizations with a small number of programs or funds; otherwise the focus on the entity as a whole can be lost.

KLT Organization
Statement of Activity [Partial]
For the Year Ended September 30, 20X2

| | Unrestricted Class | | | | Restricted Class | | 20X2 |
	Operating Fund	Board Designated	Fixed Assets	Total	Temporary	Permanent	Total
Revenues (and reclassifications)				[*Not shown here*]			
Expenses:							
Program services:							
Program development	$ 658	$ 46	$ 4	$ 708			$ 708
State and interstate services	148			148			148
Services to families	1,500	109		1,609			1,609
Special services	1,384		21	1,405			1,405
Residences for homeless men and women and senior citizens	26,026	387	366	26,779			26,779
Camping services for senior citizens, youth, and families	1,373	464	285	2,122			2,122
Community centers	8,761	794	1,423	10,978			10,978
Service extension services	1,292	34	80	1,406			1,406
Day care centers	5,873	50	6	5,929			5,929
Services to children	21,735	116	145	21,996			21,996
Total program services	68,750	2,000	2,330	73,080			73,080
Supporting services:							
Management and general	5,939	209	253	6,401			6,401
Fundraising	2,154	277	11	2,442			2,442
Total supporting services	8,093	486	264	8,843			8,843
Total expenses	76,843	2,486	2,594	81,923			81,923
Designations by governing board:							
Transfer of net assets for program services	4,834	(4,834)	—	—			—
Transfer of net assets for capital purposes	—	(3,607)	3,607	—			—
Transfer to reserves	(1,813)	1,813	—	—			—
	3,021	(6,628)	3,607	—			—
Increase in net assets	$ 269	$2,377	$ 763	$ 3,409	$ 6,926	$ 331	$10,666

The following statements illustrate a single-column presentation in the multiple statement of activity format shown as Format C in Appendix C of FASB Statement No. 117. The statement below includes only the unrestricted class and the following statement presents the details for the other two classes, plus the change in unrestricted net assets so that the total change in net assets is presented.

The GHI Foundation
Statement of Unrestricted Income and Expenses
Year Ended December 31, 20X2 and 20X1

	20X2	20X1
Income		
Dividends	$ 2,854,719	$ 2,771,309
Interest	4,016,332	3,906,590
Rent	1,603,694	1,461,627
Distribution from real estate funds	4,236,615	4,371,777
Net realized gains on investments	5,582,474	20,470,422
Increase in unrealized gains on investments	3,138,308	13,789,568
Net assets released from restriction	826,235	522,224
	22,258,377	47,293,517
Expenses		
Grant administration expense	2,160,969	2,132,248
Investment expense	2,858,146	2,782,593
Grants appropriated	16,859,156	11,342,718
Federal excise tax (refund)	(270,304)	(16,409)
Total expenses	21,607,967	16,241,150
Increase in unrestricted net assets	650,410	31,052,367
Unrestricted net assets, beginning of year	322,601,074	291,548,707
Unrestricted net assets, end of year	$323,251,484	$322,601,074

The GHI Foundation
Statement of Changes in Net Assets
Year Ended December 31, 20X2 and 20X1

	20X2	20X1
Temporarily restricted:		
Income		
Contributions	$744,356	$609,002
Investment income	102,662	98,677
Change in value of investments	34,660	150,775
Net assets released from restriction	(826,235)	(522,224)
Change in temporarily restricted net assets	55,443	336,230

	20X2	*20X1*
Permanently restricted:		
Income		
Contributions	500,000	—
Change in value of investments	15,600	27,565
Change in permanently restricted net assets	515,600	27,565
Change in unrestricted net assets	650,410	31,052,367
Change in net assets	1,221,453	31,446,162
Net assets, beginning of year	327,250,111	295,803,949
end of year	$328,471,564	$327,250,111

The following statement uses the single-column format with three net asset classes. It illustrates a reclassification out of permanently restricted net assets. Besides a correction of an error, the only event which would normally give rise to this reclassification would be the donor releasing what had originally been a permanent restriction on a gift. Note also that there is a significant amount of investment income allocated to the permanently restricted net assets, signifying that the donor intended for the corpus to grow.

JKL Foundation
Consolidated Statements of Activities
Years Ended June 30, 20X2 and 20X1

	20X2	*20X1*
Changes in Unrestricted Net Assets:		
Revenues and gains:		
Contributions	$29,241,643	$37,640,157
Investment income, net of fees	20,413,435	17,124,903
Unrealized and realized net gains on investments	15,057,219	13,479,342
Total revenues and gains	64,712,297	68,244,402
Expenses:		
Grants	32,011,140	21,162,203
Program support	1,709,432	1,414,688
Operating expenses:		
Grantmaking	1,430,404	1,613,065
Philanthropic services	102,028	121,027
Development and donor relations	1,584,094	1,303,467
Fund management	61,119	42,318
Finance, governance, and administration	559,282	494,470
Total operating expenses	3,736,927	3,574,347
Total expenses	37,457,499	26,151,238

(*continued*)

	20X2	20X1
Net increase in unrestricted net assets before reclassification	27,254,798	42,093,164
Reclassification of temporarily restricted net assets		33,908,623
Increase in unrestricted net assets	27,254,798	76,001,787
Changes in Temporarily Restricted Net Assets:		
Reclassification of permanently restricted net assets	970,722	
Reclassification of temporarily restricted net assets		(33,908,623)
Change in temporarily restricted net assets	970,722	(33,908,623)
Changes in Permanently Restricted Net Assets:		
Contributions to permanently restricted funds	7,016,911	1,753,431
Unrealized and realized net gains on investments	34,632,334	41,140,244
Reclassification of permanently restricted net assets	(970,722)	
Change in permanently restricted net assets	40,678,523	42,893,675
Increase in net assets	68,904,043	84,986,839
Net assets at beginning of year	502,927,928	417,941,089
Net assets at end of year	$571,831,971	$502,927,928

The following multicolumn format with the classes subdivided uses a less common sequence in the statement of activity.

Even before the issuance of FASB Statement No. 117, it was common among performing arts organizations (opera, symphony, ballet, and so on) to present their statements of activity in the sequential format below, which includes in the first revenue section mainly earned income, and presents all contributions below the subtotal "loss from operations." This has the effect of emphasizing the extent to which operations are subsidized by contributed income. (Some years ago, an orchestra that had calculated that box office receipts covered only 47 percent of its costs of putting on concerts, produced for fund-raising purposes a picture showing 47 percent of its musicians in concert dress, with music stands and instruments, set up in their usual positions on stage—leaving just over one-half of the stage empty. The caption under the picture read, "This is the portion of the concert that your ticket price pays for. Please contribute....")

Note the very last line, "Total increases in unrestricted net assets." This is in compliance with the requirement in paragraph 19 of FASB Statement No. 117 to present the change in net assets for each class separately, as well as in total. This statement would not comply with FASB Statement No. 117 if it were not for the final line item, "Total increases..."

This format is suitable for any organization that wishes to use it.

Sample Performing Arts Organization
Statement of Activity
Year Ended July 31, 20X2

	Unrestricted Operating Fund	Unrestricted Fixed Asset Fund	Temporarily Restricted	Permanently Restricted	Total
Operating revenues					
Opera activities					
Box office and tour	$60,454				$60,454
Media and other revenues	10,362				10,362
Ballet presentations	6,079				6,079
Interest and dividends	4,977				4,977
Net realized endowment gains applied toward authorized spending rate	3,026				3,026
Other income	1,368				1,368
Total operating revenues	86,266				86,266
Operating expenses					
Program expenses					
Opera activities					
Performances	107,180				107,180
New productions	7,393				7,393
Other expenses	1,673				1,673
Ballet presentations	6,220				6,220
	122,466				122,466
Supporting services					
Opera House	9,656	$1,063			10,719
General management	6,952	262			7,214
	16,608	1,325			17,933
Total operating expenses	139,074	1,325			140,399
Loss from operations	(52,808)	(1,325)			(54,133)
Contributions and bequests	55,410	956	$13,035	$1,636	71,037
Net assets released from restrictions					
Satisfaction of program restrictions	5,515		(5,515)		
Expiration of time restrictions	1,968		(1,968)		
	62,893	956	5,552	1,636	71,037
Fund-raising expenses	(10,008)				(10,008)
	52,885	956	5,552	1,636	61,029
Excess (deficiency) of revenues over expenses	77	(369)	5,552	1,636	6,896
Net endowment gains in excess of authorized spending rate	2,820				2,820
Pension adjustment	2,060				2,060
Interfund transfers	356	(356)			
Change in net assets	5,313	(725)	5,552	1,636	11,776
Net assets					
Beginning of year	18,930	18,485	29,047	73,795	140,257
End of year	$24,243	$17,760	$34,599	$75,431	$152,033
Total increase in unrestricted net assets					$ 4,588

This combining statement shows two movements of net assets between parts of the organization: one to reflect the transfer of assets and net assets from one organizational unit to another, and the other to reclassify some unrestricted net assets to the permanently restricted class to comply with a donor's stipulation that a permanently restricted challenge gift be met with a matching amount of unrestricted resources.

To be in conformity with paragraph 19 of FASB Statement No. 117, the total change in unrestricted net assets should be shown as demonstrated in the previous example.

The BCD Foundation
Combining Statement of Activity
Year Ended December 31, 20X2

	The BCD Foundation				[Affliliated] Foundation	
	Unrestricted	Temporarily Restricted	Permanently Restricted	Total	Unrestricted	Total
Revenues, gains, and support:						
Contributions	$21,505		$20,000	$ 41,505		$ 41,505
Investment income, net of investment fees	12,661		392	13,053	$510	13,563
Changes in the value of charitable trusts		$99	384	483		483
Other income	37			37		37
Total revenues, gains, and support	34,203	99	20,776	55,078	510	55,588
Expenses:						
Grants	3,452			3,452	1,109	4,561
Program-related expenses:						
Grant-making expenses	184			184	142	326
Special projects and other	536			536		536
	720			720	142	862
Supporting services:						
Management and general	303			303	35	338
Development	117			117		117
	420			420	35	455
Total expenses	4,592			4,592	1,286	5,878
Change in net assets before transfer and reclassification	29,611	99	20,776	50,486	(776)	49,710
Transfer of net assets	(3,378)			(3,378)	3,378	
Reclassification to match challenge grant	(5,000)		5,000			
Change in net assets after transfer and reclassification	21,233	99	25,776	47,108	2,602	49,710
Net assets, beginning of year	73,846	1,655	6,304	81,805		81,805
Net assets, end of year	$95,079	$1,754	$32,080	$128,913	$2,602	$131,515

Total increase in unrestricted net assets $23,835

This organization acts as a recipient organization for a significant portion of its campaign proceeds.

Community Foundation of ABC County
Statement of Activities (Campaign Section)
Year Ended June 30, 20X2

	Unrestricted	Temporarily Restricted	Total
Revenues, gains, and other support			
Gross campaign results for 20X2	$ 904,694		$ 904,694
Less donor designations	(161,019)		(161,019)
Less State Employees Federated Appeal (SEFA) designations	(66,925)		(66,925)
Total campaign for 20X2	676,750		676,750
Less provision for uncollectible pledges	(55,328)		(55,328)
Net campaign revenue for 20X2	621,422		621,422
Gross campaign results for 20X3		$7,100	7,100

CAPTION SEQUENCES

This organization puts operating expenses above operating revenues. This has the effect of putting at the top of the statement the numbers which best reflect the organization's programmatic efforts for the year. See also the Sample Performing Arts Organization on page 26.

CDE Performing Arts Center
Combined Statements of Activity [Unrestricted class only]
Years Ended June 30, 20X2 and 20X1

	20X2	20X1
Change in unrestricted net assets:		
Operations:		
Expenses:		
[*Center*] sponsored events	$ 11,685,874	10,824,709
Hall rental operations	7,633,907	7,451,361
Real estate operations	5,488,248	5,154,199
Youth education programs	1,279,158	1,235,323
Other operations and special projects	1,520,789	1,700,351
General and administrative	2,965,226	2,768,416
	30,573,202	29,134,359

(*continued*)

Revenues:	20X2	20X1
Box office receipts from [Center] sponsored events	8,246,980	7,626,089
Hall rental operations	5,341,243	5,131,300
Real estate operations	5,415,871	5,285,799
Other income	723,877	653,507
Net assets released from restrictions	806,325	658,683
	20,534,296	19,355,378
Excess of operating expenses over operating revenues	(10,038,906)	(9,778,981)
Nonoperating revenues (expenses):		
Annual campaign and fund-raising events	7,546,596	6,620,454
The [City] and other government agency grants	1,151,698	1,054,516
Investment income, net	4,014,399	2,093,302
Fund-raising expenses	(2,807,654)	(2,685,877)
	9,905,039	7,082,395
Decrease in unrestricted net assets	(133,867)	(2,696,586)

Since the temporarily restricted net asset class accounts for the great majority of this organization's revenues, it is placed first in the following single-column format (although this is not a required format).

TRC Foundation
Statement of Activities [Revenue section]

	20X2	20X1
Years Ended December 31,		
Changes in temporarily restricted net assets:		
Contributions	$ 9,141,829	$ 9,306,386
Reclassifications—net assets released from restrictions	(8,990,430)	(9,317,707)
Change in temporarily restricted net assets	151,399	(11,321)
Changes in unrestricted net assets:		
Revenues:		
Contributions	151,084	80,768
Investment income	301,870	500,729
Field revenue—sales, rentals, and other	403,612	433,383
Other income	169,848	68,100
	1,026,414	1,082,980
Reclassifications—net assets released from restriction by satisfaction of purpose restrictions	8,990,430	9,317,707
Total unrestricted revenues and reclassifications	$ 10,016,844	$10,400,687

Some organizations make periodic internal "assessments" against restricted and designated funds to cover the costs of administering those funds. This practice must be disclosed to donors. This disclosure, which should be made in the fund-raising appeal, is not a requirement of generally accepted accounting principles (GAAP), as GAAP does not deal with matters outside the financial statements. It is referred to here for information only. One might consider it an ethical requirement. These assessments may be shown as in the following example.

Note that the assessments are initially reported in the temporarily restricted column and then reclassified to the unrestricted column. It could be argued that because donors are presumed to be aware of the fact that a portion of their gifts will be used for activities (that is, administration) other than the stated purpose of the gifts, that amount is initially unrestricted and should be reported as such. The totals would not change, but the "Assessments" line under "Reclassifications" would disappear.

BTL Organization
Statement of Activities [Revenue section]
Year Ended December 31, 20X2

	Unrestricted	Temporarily Restricted
Support and revenues:		
Contributions	$ 261,936	$ 121,754
Affiliate support	199,728	—
Special events	33,147	—
Investment income	7,533	4,450
Rental, fees, and other	21,713	—
	524,057	126,204
Reclassifications:		
Assessments against restricted gifts	25,241	(25,241)
Net assets released from restriction by satisfaction of purpose restrictions	107,232	(107,232)
Total support, revenues, and reclassifications	$ 656,530	$ (6,269)

Foundations tend to use many different formats with regard to the sequence of certain items. This grant-making organization presents realized investment gains with other income and grants and excise tax with other expenses. Note that the excise tax is considered an investment expense and thus is partly netted against the related investment income.

PQR Foundation
Statements of Operations and Changes in Unrestricted Net Assets
For the Years Ended December 31, 20X2 and 20X1

	20X2	*20X1*
INCOME		
Real estate revenues	$ 61,095	$ 55,812
Marketable securities	93,188	108,616
Private entity investments	6,164	7,154
Investment management expenses	(61,050)	(63,922)
	99,397	107,660
REALIZED GAINS		
Marketable securities	266,763	197,749
Private equity investments	26,798	5,966
Real estate investments	84,509	2,984
	378,070	206,699
Total income and realized gains	477,467	314,359
GRANTS AND OTHER EXPENSES		
Grants approved	145,407	158,196
Program-related expenses	2,694	2,918
Administrative expenses	25,995	22,211
Excise taxes	4,921	3,848
	179,017	187,173
Results of operations before unrealized appreciation on investments	298,450	127,186
Increase (decrease) in unrealized appreciation on investments (net of federal excise tax of $2,743 in 20X2 and $261 in 20X1):		
Marketable securities	66,146	(1,556)
Private equity investments	34,309	513
Real estate investments	33,911	1,130
	134,366	87
Increase in unrestricted net assets	432,816	127,273
NET ASSETS, beginning of year	3,164,602	3,037,329
NET ASSETS, end of year	$3,597,418	$3,164,602

This grant-making organization presents all investment gains with other income, grants in a separate section, and excise tax with other expenses.

STU Foundation
Statements of Income, Expenses, and Changes in Unrestricted Net Assets

	Year Ended June 30,	
	20X2	*20X1*
INCOME		
Dividends	$ 2,244,135	$ 2,230,620
Interest	2,607,105	2,409,908
Change in value of marketable securities	33,237,772	32,923,430
	38,089,012	37,563,958
GRANTS MADE	8,800,804	5,390,700
OTHER EXPENSES		
Investment advisory fees	467,680	403,751
Operating expenses	372,128	342,082
Federal excise tax	114,327	209,560
Pension	117,044	91,462
Legal, accounting, and other professional fees	59,335	49,799
	1,130,514	1,096,654
Excess of income over grants and expenses	28,157,694	31,076,604
Unrestricted net assets:		
Beginning of year	159,975,781	128,899,177
End of year	$188,133,475	$159,975,781

This grant-making organization presents all investment gains below income and expenses, excise tax is deducted from other income, and grants are presented with other expenses. Note that the excise tax is considered an investment expense and thus is partly netted against the related investment income.

VWX Foundation
Statement of Activities
Years Ended December 31, 20X2 and 20X1

	20X2	*20X1*
Investment Income:		
Interest	$ 9,221,450	$ 8,372,881
Dividends	5,304,901	4,130,451
	14,526,351	12,503,332
Investment expenses and federal excise taxes	(1,707,248)	(1,395,277)
Net investment income	12,819,103	11,108,055

(continued)

	20X2	20X1
Grants and Expenses:		
Grants, net of cancellations	16,169,090	14,364,916
Grant administration and other program management expenses	2,990,057	2,676,908
General administration	868,400	672,677
	20,027,547	17,714,501
Decrease in net assets before investment gains	(7,208,444)	(6,606,446)
Net Investment Gains:		
Net realized gain on sales of investments	36,179,678	24,321,341
Increase in unrealized appreciation in fair value of investments, net of deferred tax expense of $352,318 and $211,240 in 20X2 and 20X1, respectively	17,263,589	10,350,759
Net investment gains	53,443,267	34,672,100
Increase in unrestricted net assets	46,234,823	28,065,654
Unrestricted net assets at beginning of year	351,354,562	323,288,908
Unrestricted net assets at end of year	$397,589,385	$351,354,562

This club shows a summary of departmental profit or loss directly on the face of the statement of activity. Note that functional expense allocations would be presented in a note.

The EFG Club, Inc.
Statement of Revenues, Expenses, and Changes in Net Assets
Year Ended March 31, 20X2

	Sales and Services	Costs and Expenses	Net	
Revenues:				
Dues				$1,508
Initiation fees				535
Departmental operations:				
Rooms	$ 506	$ 175	$331	
Food	3,401	2,947	454	
Beverages	848	492	356	
Other	113	88	25	
	$4,868	$ 3,702		1,166
Net departmental revenues and general revenue				3,209
Other expenses:				
General				1,396
Depreciation				205
Taxes				462

	Sales and Services	Costs and Expenses	Net
Utilities			512
Repairs			199
Retirement plan			165
Total other expenses			2,939
Excess of revenues over expenses			270
Members' equity (net assets), beginning of year			5,370
Members' equity (net assets), end of year			$5,640

· ·

This research organization uses an operating measure that includes an investment return in operations as the result of a spending policy, but has an overall negative (loss) investment return. (Only the Total column of the statement of activities is presented).

ABC Institute for Research
Statement of Activities
Year Ended December 31, 20X2

Operating revenues and other support	
Research grants and contracts	$ 7,013,811
Investment income allocated to operations	4,246,000
Contributed facilities and services	2,242,600
Contributions, royalties, and other revenues	959,553
Total operating revenues and other support	14,461,964
Operating expenses	
Program services	
Research	10,159,186
Greenhouse and other services	932,209
Nonresearch	194,762
Total program services	11,286,157
Supporting services	
Administration	1,494,028
Fund raising	254,750
Total operating expenses	13,034,935
Change in net assets from operations	1,427,029
Investment income (loss) allocated to nonoperating revenues	(9,394,512)
Loss on disposal of fixed assets	(41,965)
Change in net assets	(8,009,448)
Net assets—beginning of year	79,496,166
Net assets—end of year	71,486,718

OTHER MATTERS

This statement of activity includes budgeted amounts and variances. Note that since the expenses shown here are by natural category, and since this is a voluntary health and welfare organization, a separate statement of functional expenses (or a note showing the same information as in such a statement) would be required.

QRS Charity
Statement of Revenues, Expenses,
and Changes in Unrestricted Net Assets—Budget vs. Actual

	Year Ended March 31, 20X2		
	Actual	*Budget*	*Variance Favorable (Unfavorable)*
Revenues:			
Federal grant	$ 769,000	$ 943,000	$(173,000)
Net patient service revenue	215,000	258,000	(43,000)
Contributions—unrestricted	57,000	25,000	32,000
[*State*] [*Disease*] Council	1,000	—	1,000
United Way	2,000	5,000	(3,000)
Total revenues, net of patient services deductions	1,044,000	1,231,000	(186,000)
Expenses:			
Personnel	412,000	445,000	33,000
Contractual patient care	308,000	415,000	107,000
Supplies	78,000	100,000	22,000
Fringe benefits	68,000	75,000	7,000
Travel	17,000	19,000	2,000
Rent	50,000	44,000	(6,000)
Insurance	17,000	22,000	5,000
Utilities	9,000	13,000	4,000
Equipment rental	36,000	38,000	2,000
Patient transportation	3,000	4,000	1,000
Repairs and maintenance	9,000	8,000	(1,000)
Publications	6,000	3,000	(3,000)
Telephone	5,000	6,000	1,000
Professional fees	9,000	9,000	—
Miscellaneous	42,000	22,000	(20,000)
Total expenses	1,069,000	1,223,000	154,000
Excess of net (expenses) revenues	(25,000)		
Unrestricted net assets:			
At beginning of year	28,000		
At end of year	$ 3,000		

This club presents additional information about its various profit centers, both in dollars and percentages, as separate schedules. The schedule for one profit center is illustrated. Some clubs present such details in a note.

The EFG Club, Inc.
Beverage Department

| | Year Ended December 31, | | | |
	20X2	20X1	20X2	20X1
	Amount		Percent	
Gross beverage sales	$ 904,000	$ 638,000	87.6	87.1
Beverage service charge	127,000	94,000	12.4	12.9
Total revenues	1,031,000	732,000	100.0	100.0
Less cost of sales	232,000	174,000	22.5	23.8
Gross profit	799,000	558,000	77.5	76.2
Departmental expenses:				
Payroll and related expenses:				
Salaries and wages	233,000	195,000	22.6	26.6
Payroll taxes	18,000	14,000	1.8	2.0
Employees' meals	3,000	4,000	.3	.5
Employee benefits	13,000	10,000	1.3	1.4
Total payroll and related expenses	267,000	223,000	26.0	30.5
Other expenses:				
Bar expense	13,000	12,000	1.3	1.7
Bar food	40,000	27,000	3.9	3.9
Glassware	13,000	11,000	1.3	1.5
License	1,000	1,000	—	.1
Miscellaneous	2,000	3,000	.2	.4
Printing and stationery	4,000	6,000	.5	.9
Uniforms	16,000	11,000	1.6	1.5
Total departmental expenses	356,000	294,000	34.6	40.1
Total cost of sales and departmental expenses	588,000	468,000	57.1	63.9
Beverage department income	$ 443,000	$ 264,000	42.9	36.1

Proceeds from special events must be shown gross of direct benefits expense, per paragraphs 13.21 and 13.22 of the Audit and Accounting Guide *Not-for-Profit Organizations* (the Guide), but the expenses may be shown in the expense section of the statement, or may be shown as in the following example. (Reporting net amounts is permitted, but not required, if the receipts and related costs result from special events that are peripheral or incidental activities.)

YTL Organization
Statement of Activities [Unrestricted revenue section]
Year Ended June 30, 20X2

	Unrestricted
Public support and revenues:	
Public support:	
Contributions	$ 16,587,739
Special events:	
Proceeds	31,603,213
Less: Direct expenses	(7,753,443)
Transfers from affiliates	2,100,861
Total public support	42,538,370

•••••••••••••••••••••••

In contrast, investment income may be shown gross or net of expenses (per paragraph 13.27 of the Guide), but if shown net, the amount of expenses must be disclosed, either as a deduction in the manner shown above, in a note, or as part of the revenue caption, as follows.

Revenue:	
Other revenue	$ 1,650,000
Investment income, net of expenses of $24,750 etc.	236,000

•••••••••••••••••••••••

A note (probably part of a longer note) would be as follows.

Note X: Investment Income

Investment income as reported is net of related expenses of $24,750.

CHAPTER 3: Sample Statements of Cash Flows

The Financial Accounting Standards Board (FASB) Statement of Financial Accounting Standards No. 117, *Financial Statements of Not-for-Profit Organizations* (paragraph 147, consistent with paragraph 27 of FASB Statement No. 95, Statement of Cash Flows), encourages, but does not require, organizations to use the direct method in preparing the statement of cash flows. Further discussion of this issue is in that paragraph, and in other sources referenced therein. Both the direct and indirect methods are illustrated in the following examples.

Note that disclosures regarding noncash financing and investing activities are required. Examples of such noncash activities are donations of securities, land and buildings, assumption of a mortgage, and other comparable activities.

Note also that contributions restricted for long-term purposes, such as permanent endowments and the acquisition of property and equipment, are considered financing activities. If the indirect method is used, such contributions should be deducted from operating activities (accrual basis) and added to financing activities (cash basis).

DIRECT METHOD

MNP Foundation
Consolidated Statements of Cash Flows
Years Ended June 30, 20X2 and 20X1

	20X2	20X1
Cash flows from operating activities:		
Cash received from contributions	$ 29,241,643	$37,840,167
Interest and dividends received, net of fees	19,936,243	17,168,553
Grants paid	(29,557,744)	(21,270,598)
Taxes paid	(400,000)	(300,000)
Cash paid:		
For other program expenses	(1,709,432)	(1,414,688)
To employees and suppliers	(3,570,203)	(3,544,809)
Net cash provided by operating activities	13,940,507	29,078,625
Cash flows from investing activities:		
Proceeds from sale of investments	726,976,859	628,274,690
Purchases of investments	(749,407,732)	(657,835,849)
Purchases of equipment	(212,767)	(92,723)
Proceeds from investments in notes receivable	209,834	197,844
Net cash used by investing activities	(22,433,826)	(29,456,038)

(*continued*)

	20X2	20X1
Cash flows from financing activities:		
Contributions to permanently restricted endowment funds	6,638,366	1,817,315
Contributions to charitable remainder unitrusts	450,000	
Payments to life tenants of charitable unitrusts	(71,455)	(63,884)
Net cash provided by financing activities	7,016,911	1,753,431
Net change in cash	(1,476,408)	1,376,018
Cash, beginning of year	1,612,678	236,660
Cash, end of year	$ 136,270	$1,612,678

FGH University
Statement of Cash Flows
Years Ended July 31, 20X2 and 20X1

	20X2	20X1
Cash flow from operating activities:		
Tuition, fees, sales, and services of auxiliary enterprises	$ 521,184	$483,330
Investment income	155,366	139,991
Gifts, grants, and contracts	696,657	634,328
Receipts in agency accounts held for others	88,469	72,886
Cash paid to suppliers and employees	(1,202,374)	(1,112,936)
Disbursements from agency accounts	(89,221)	(71,500)
Interest paid	(39,350)	(38,477)
Net cash provided by operating activities	130,731	107,622
Cash flow from investing activities:		
Land, building, and equipment purchases	(171,042)	(147,147)
Student, faculty, and other loans:		
New loans made	(27,709)	(22,445)
Principal collected	18,822	20,290
Purchases of investments	(2,488,892)	(2,979,991)
Sales of investments	2,363,125	2,829,983
Security lending collateral returned	34,192	(4,685)
Net cash used for investing activities	(271,504)	(303,995)
Cash flow from financing activities:		
Gifts for endowment, capital projects, and student loans	109,674	133,478
Receipts under split-interest gift arrangements	100,000	
Income reinvested in endowment, capital projects, and student loans	20,137	6,765
Proceeds from borrowing	82,939	8,775
Repayment of debt	(14,630)	(25,827)

		20X2	20X1
Net cash provided by financing activities		298,120	123,191
Increase (decrease) in cash and cash equivalents		157,347	(73,182)
Cash and cash equivalents, beginning of year		159,041	232,223
Cash and cash equivalents, end of year	$	316,388	$159,041
Noncash investing and financing activities:			
Receipt of donated fixed assets	$	11,715	$ 18,000
Assumption of mortgage on donated fixed assets		2,040	
Donated investment securities		55,100	31,850

When the direct method is used to prepare the statement of cash flows, the required reconciliation of the change in net assets to net cash flows from operating activities may be shown as part of the statement of cash flows, or it may be shown in a separate schedule (per paragraph 119 of FASB Statement No. 95, reprinted in FASB Statement No. 117, paragraph 147). This schedule may be included in a note to the financial statements if desired, as shown in the following sample note.

Note X: Cash Flow Reconciliation

The change in University net assets is reconciled to net cash provided by operations as follows:

	20X2	20X1
Change in net assets	$ 762,671	$ 523,155
(Increase) in [Affiliate] net equity	(39,414)	(8,923)
Depreciation and retirement of fixed assets	140,926	94,889
Increase in accounts payable	67,121	39,857
(Increase) decrease in accounts receivable	(10,512)	6,158
(Increase) in inventories and prepaid expenses	(4,949)	(8,490)
(Increase) decrease in contributions receivable	20,789	(80,779)
Gifts, grants, and reinvested income of student loan, endowment, and plant net assets	(251,219)	(129,904)
Actuarial adjustment related to split-interest gifts	968	10,385
Realized and unrealized gains on investments	(555,650)	(338,706)
Net cash provided by operating activities	$ 130,731	$ 107,622

•••••••••••••••••••••••

The following example illustrates an investing cash flows section showing subtotal of investment activity.

The BCD Foundation
Statement of Cash Flows [Partial]
Year Ended December 31, 20X2

	The BCD Foundation	[Affiliated] Foundation	Total
Cash flows from investing activities:			
Payments for investments purchased	(197,723,450)	(1,123,524)	(198,846,974)
Received from sale of investments	141,437,801	1,939,636	143,377,437
Net (increase) decrease in investments	(56,285,649)	816,112	(55,469,537)
Principal payments received on program-related loans receivable	442,880		442,880
Disbursements to borrowers under program-related loans	(309,609)		(309,609)
Purchase of furniture and equipment	(10,549)		(10,549)
Net cash provided by (used in) investing activities	(56,162,927)	816,112	(55,346,815)

INDIRECT METHOD

Note that contributions and other income which are permanently restricted are shown as a deduction from the change in net assets to come to cash flows from operations. Also note that this deduction may not equal the corresponding addition in the financing section; this is because the first is an accrual basis item, while the second is cash basis.

Art Museum
Consolidated Statement of Cash Flows
For the Year Ended June 30, 20X2

Cash flows from operating activities:	
Change in net assets	$ 69,624
Adjustments to reconcile change in net assets to net cash provided by operating activities:	
Depreciation	2,982
Net realized and unrealized gains on long-term investments	(38,565)
Decrease in accounts receivable	7
(Increase) in contributions and grants receivable	(16,155)
Decrease in accrued investment income and other receivables	132
(Increase) in inventories	(1,553)
(Increase) in prepaid expenses and deferred charges	(961)
Increase in accounts payable, accrued expenses, and other liabilities	6,431
(Decrease) in deferred revenue	(1,623)

Contributions and net investment income restricted for long-term investment	(2,001)
Sales of works of art	(8,127)
Acquisition of works of art	22,488
Contributions and net investment income restricted for capital acquisition and construction	(23,151)
Net cash provided by operating activities	9,594

Cash flows from investing activities:

Purchase of property, plant, and equipment	(24,128)
Sales of investments	267,319
Purchase of investments	(277,067)
Sales of works of art	8,127
Acquisition of works of art	(22,488)
Net cash used by investing activities	(48,237)

Cash flows from financing activities:

Proceeds from sales of works of art:	
Investment in endowment	70
Contributions and net investment income restricted for:	
Capital acquisition and construction	23,381
Investment in endowment	2,001
Borrowings under mortgages and loans payable	11,000
Repayments on mortgages and loans payable	(1,746)
Net cash provided by financing activities	34,706
Net (decrease) in cash and cash equivalents	(3,937)
Cash and cash equivalents at beginning of year	15,193
Cash and cash equivalents at end of year	$ 11,256

CHAPTER 4: Sample Statements of Functional Expenses

A statement of functional expenses is a required statement for not-for-profit organizations that are voluntary health and welfare organizations. Voluntary health and welfare organizations are defined in the AICPA Audit and Accounting Guide *Not-for-Profit Organizations* (the Guide) as "…organizations that derive their revenue primarily from voluntary contributions from the general public…." The term "general public" excludes government entities.

Organizations have great flexibility as to how many program and supporting service columns and how many lines are shown on the statements. However, the columns reflected by voluntary health and welfare organizations should be the same as the functional expense line items in the statement of activities.

The first illustrated example is typical. See also Chapter 7, under "Expenses." Various formats are used in practice to show comparative information. The ones illustrated are the most popular; others include showing comparative totals at the bottom of the statement in addition to or in place of the right-hand column. Alternatively, a complete prior-year statement can be presented, and must be if the organization is a voluntary health and welfare organization and the auditor intends to express an opinion on both years. Some organizations combine all payroll expenses (salaries, employee benefits, payroll taxes) into one line.

[See statement on page 44.]

Statement of Functional Expenses for the Year Ended August 31, 20X2
(With Comparative Totals for 20X1)

	Program Services				Supporting Services		Total Program and Supporting Services	
	Research	Education	Patient Services	Community Services	Management and General	Fund Raising	20X2	20X1
Awards and grants	$70,620	$ 6,316	$ 350	$ 867	$ —	$ —	$ 78,153	$ 73,713
Salaries	2,732	29,656	13,337	7,848	9,771	18,076	81,420	74,715
Employee benefits	345	4,384	1,952	1,122	1,417	2,466	11,686	6,008
Payroll taxes	165	2,417	1,068	620	1,136	1,380	6,786	11,780
Professional fees	72	643	89	169	2,092	1,638	4,703	4,356
Supplies	142	1,678	630	394	568	1,218	4,630	4,352
Telephone	141	1,964	866	532	622	1,606	5,731	5,089
Postage and shipping	94	3,012	920	519	616	2,999	8,160	7,645
Occupancy	687	5,033	2,259	1,237	1,495	2,521	13,232	11,588
Information processing	256	1,063	461	272	662	1,549	4,263	3,858
Printing and publications	115	9,541	1,087	936	512	4,886	17,077	14,517
Meetings and conferences	739	4,010	1,044	1,046	1,088	2,166	10,093	9,818
Other travel	199	2,203	764	558	785	1,192	5,701	5,436
Specific assistance to individuals	—	—	9,848	540	—	—	10,388	9,772
Other expenses	51	693	284	379	913	904	3,224	2,853
Depreciation	734	2,363	935	594	919	1,132	6,677	5,119
Total expenses	$77,092	$74,976	$35,894	$17,633	$22,596	$43,733	$271,924	$250,619

Some organizations display in their statement of functional expenses information about interdepartmental charges and the allocation of a pool of direct overhead expenses to other functions. This appears as in the following example (the format of the top part of the statement is as shown in the previous example).

This is a membership organization which solicits new and renewing memberships rather than contributions. Its second supporting service is, accordingly, called member development.

| | Program | | Support | | |
	Education	Research	Management	Member Development	Total
Salaries	$	$	$	$	$
Utilities					
[*Etc.*]					
Miscellaneous					
Interdepartmental charges	(10)	63	(148)	95	—
Subtotal	3,421	9,966	5,214	2,069	20,670
Allocation of direct supporting services	356	1,443	(2,542)	743	—
Total	$3,777	$11,409	$ 2,672	$2,812	$20,670

This organization has so many different functions and subtotals that presenting them in two "layers" rather than all side-by-side is a practical way to avoid either crowding the numbers or using a fold-out page.

CRA Charity
Statement of Functional Expenses
For the Year Ended June 30, 20X2, With Comparative Totals for 20X1

| | Program Services | | | | | Total |
	Family Services	Disaster Relief	Elderly Services	Community Services	Youth Services	Total Program Services
Salaries and wages	$43	$ 28	$286	$ 46	$26	$ 429
Employee benefits	7	4	45	7	4	67
Total	50	32	331	53	30	496
Travel	3	4	16	4	5	32
Equipment maintenance and rental	3	2	12	2	1	20
Supplies and materials	2	4	128	18	3	155
Contractual services	10	14	139	18	11	192
Financial and material assistance	5	44	12	5	9	75
Total before depreciation	73	100	638	100	59	970
Depreciation of buildings and equipment	2	3	26	3	3	37
Total expenses	$75	$103	$664	$103	$62	$1,007

| | Supporting Services | | | Total | | |
| | Membership and Fund Raising | Management and General | Total Supporting Services | Program Services (as above) | Totals | |
					20X2	20X1
Salaries and wages	$13	$30	$43	$ 429	$ 472	$428
Employee benefits	2	5	7	67	74	69
Total	15	35	50	496	546	497
Travel	1	5	6	32	38	33
Equipment maintenance and rental		1	1	20	21	21
Supplies and materials	1	5	6	155	161	147
Contractual services	12	14	26	192	218	180
Financial and material assistance	1	1	2	75	77	75
Total before depreciation	30	61	91	970	1,061	953
Depreciation of buildings and equipment	1	2	3	37	40	39
Total expenses	$31	$63	$94	$1,007	$1,101	$992

CHAPTER 5: Sample Disclosures—General

Note that these sample notes are not necessarily complete for any given organization's circumstances. Also, the sample notes included in this publication are generally limited to those for which the fact that the organization is a not-for-profit organization introduces unique or different reporting or disclosure requirements or both. Notes which do not differ based on the type of organization, such as pension disclosures required by Financial Accounting Standards Board (FASB) Statement of Financial Accounting Standards No. 87, *Employers' Accounting for Pensions*, and capital leases (FASB Statement No. 13, *Accounting for Leases*), are generally not included.

In practice, notes that include descriptions of accounting policies are often gathered together in one "Accounting Policies" note. Some or all of them are, however, sometimes included in other notes that include additional information about the item in question. For example, the organization's accounting policies related to fixed assets and depreciation may be presented in the note that summarizes fixed assets by type.

DESCRIPTION OF ORGANIZATION AND GENERAL ACCOUNTING POLICIES

Paragraph 13.31 of the AICPA Audit and Accounting Guide *Not-for-Profit Organizations* (the Guide) requires the financial statements to provide a description of the nature of the organization's activities, including a description of each of its major classes of programs, either on the statement of activities or in the notes to the financial statements. Some organizations combine these two items into one note; others put them in two separate notes.

Note X: Basis of Presentation

The Foundation follows the requirements of Financial Accounting Standards Board (FASB) Statement of Financial Accounting Standards No. 117, *Financial Statements of Not-For-Profit Organizations*. Under FASB Statement No. 117, the Foundation is required to report information regarding its financial position and activities according to three classes of net assets: unrestricted net assets, temporarily restricted net assets, and permanently restricted net assets.

Additionally, the Foundation follows the recommendation made by a special committee of industry experts, the FASB Committee of the Fiscal and Administrative Officers Group (FAOG) of the Council of Foundations, set forth in a position report, Report on Classification of Net Assets by Community Foundations (the FAOG Report), issued in September 1997. FAOG recommends that net assets of community foundations should generally be classified as unrestricted with certain limited exceptions. Funds subject to time restrictions, including most split-interest arrangements, should be classified in temporarily restricted net assets. Funds should be classified in permanently restricted net assets only when both of the following conditions are met:

- The donor gift instrument does not permit invasion of the principal, and
- The governing documents of the community foundations do not provide for the invasion of corpus.

....

[*Note that the treatment of endowment gains in this example is not common. The more common treatment is shown later, in Note X: Endowment, on page 56.*]

Note X: Summary of Significant Accounting Policies

In-kind contributions consisted of goods and services for which $261,000 has been reflected in the financial statements for the year ended May 31, 20X2. Additionally, volunteers have donated significant amounts of time to the Association in various capacities. However, these services have not been reflected in the financial statements since they neither require specialized skills nor would have been typically purchased had they not been donated. The value of these services is not readily determinable.

Restricted endowment net assets are so stipulated by the donor and consist of the original principal to be held in perpetuity and the related gains and losses (realized and unrealized) thereon. The Board and legal counsel have interpreted [*State*] law, in effect at May 31, 20X2, as requiring permanent retention of the gains on restricted endowment funds and those gains are recorded as permanently restricted net assets.

[*Note that the preceding paragraph is based on an interpretation of state law. In many states that have adopted the Uniform Management of Institutional Funds Act (UMIFA), organizations more commonly recognize investment gains from restricted endowment funds in the unrestricted class of net assets, unless the donor has specified otherwise.*]

Charitable perpetual trusts consist of funds administered outside of the Association in which the Association has the irrevocable right to receive the income earned on the trust assets in perpetuity, but never receives the assets held in trust.

Note X: Fluctuations in Revenues and Expenses

Due to the emphasis of the Organization's programs on provision of disaster relief, the level of Organization activity normally varies from year to year by a considerable amount, depending on the number of incidents occurring which cause people to need the Organization's help. In 20X2 there were a significantly higher number of such incidents, and, accordingly, expenses were higher than in 20X1, and additional funds were raised to cover the increased expenses and to rebuild the Organization's reserves for future disasters.

....

Note X: Nature of Organization

The Ballet Association (the Association) is a nonprofit corporation organized in 1972. The Association stages several major ballets each year, operates a ballet school, and promotes public interest in the art of ballet. The mission of the Association is to be a premier cultural asset esteemed in the community and the world of dance for:

* Inspired performances which engage discerning audiences at home or on tour;
* A school which trains future dancers and nurtures passion, creativity, and discipline in every child who attends;
* A solid financial base which supports artistic innovation while ensuring long-range stability;
* Integrity in human relationships, without which other achievements are incomplete;
* Dedicated artists, teachers, students, staff, trustees, audience members, and supporters, who all find their lives enhanced by their sharing in this enterprise.

....

Note X: Nature of Organization and Significant Accounting Policies

Organization and Basis of Presentation

The accompanying consolidated financial statements present the consolidated financial position, changes in net assets, and cash flows of the Organization. All significant intra-organizational accounts and transactions have been eliminated. The Organization has national and international programs that are conducted by its headquarters (national sector) operations and various affiliates discussed below. These consolidated financial statements also include the net assets and operations of [*Company*] Ltd., a 100%-owned captive subsidiary.

Nature of Organization

The [*Denomination*] Church Corporation (DCC) is a [*State*] corporation formed in 19T8 as the church's world headquarters. The corporation is a nonprofit religious organization exempt from income tax under Section 501(c)(3) of the U.S. Internal Revenue Code. The [*Denomination*] Church of Canada is a Canadian charity formed in June 19V4 and is exempt from income tax under Section 149(l)(f) of the Income Tax Act of Canada. The DCC and the [*Denomination*] Church of Canada participate in a joint effort to administer and promote the purposes and activities of the denomination.

The financial statements of The DCC include the operations of the following entities for which control and economic interests exist:

- The following 501(c)(3) tax exempt, liberal arts colleges and universities, with June 30 fiscal year ends:
  — [*College*] in [*State*],
  — [*Bible College*] in Canada (tax exempt under the provisions of the Income Tax Act in Canada),
  — [*College*] in [*State*], including its affiliates, [*School*] and the [*School*] Foundation, and
  — [*Denomination*] University in [*State*], including its affiliate, the [*Denomination*] Retirement Center, a 501(c)(3) tax-exempt, elderly care facility consisting of [*Health Care Center*] and [*Retirement Apartments*].

- [*Denomination*] Investment Foundation is a 501(c)(3) tax-exempt corporation (August 31 fiscal year end) organized to loan funds to member churches and other church-related organizations of The DCC located throughout the United States and abroad for various building programs.

- [*Denomination*] Indian Ministries is a 501(c)(3) tax-exempt, corporation (June 30 fiscal year end) organized to promote, develop, and supervise the evangelization to the Indian peoples.

- [*Children's Home*], Inc. is a 501(c)(3) tax-exempt organization (June 30 fiscal year end) which provides a residential program for children from ages 6 to 17 who are dependent, neglected, or abused.

Principles of Consolidation

The financial statements of DCC include all activities conducted through its International Headquarters and the subsidiary entities described above. The International Headquarters' activity includes:

- Operations of The [*Denomination*] Church of Canada.
- Receipt of United Stewardship Fund and Educational Institution Fund remittances from church districts.
- Receipt of other funds from church districts and individuals, including support for World Missions missionaries and projects.
- Disbursement of home office department budgeted and restricted funds.
- Disbursement of Educational Institution Fund contributions to the denomination's institutions of higher education based on an approved formula (these transactions are eliminated from the combined financial statements).
- Operations of [*Press*] and [*Denomination*] Women International.
- Receipts and disbursements of World Missions foreign fields such as hospitals, schools, and other such revenue-producing activities.

DCC does not include the operations of the local [*Denomination*] churches and corresponding districts due to the control structure of those entities. The statements also do not include the [*Denomination*] Pension Fund, Inc., as provided by generally accepted accounting principles.

Trust Funds and Funds Held for Others

Trust agreements administered include revocable trusts, irrevocable trusts, charitable remainder annuity trusts and unitrusts, and charitable lead trusts. (Trusts held for others are reported as liabilities—funds held for others. Trusts are reported as part liabilities as described in Note [*number*] and part net assets as disclosed in Note [*number*]. The net assets portion represents the present value of future irrevocable cash flows due the Organization.)

Funds held for others include those administered as an agent for other committees, agencies, and institutions. The types of funds include endowments, annuities, charitable remainder trusts, revocable trusts, and other funds as described in Note [*number*].

The Organization administers the following types of funds for its own operations and as an agent for others:

Charitable Gift Annuities

Annuity agreements are issued in exchange for a payment that constitutes part charitable contribution and part purchase of an annuity, providing for payments to the stated annuitant(s) during their lifetime(s). These agreements constitute a general obligation of the Organization. (The gift portion of annuities and investment reserves in excess of liabilities are reported as net assets. Annuities administered for others are included in funds held for others.)

Advise and Consult Funds

Charitable fund agreements allow donors to make outright charitable contributions to a fund which is used to provide charitable donations to qualified organizations. The funds are under the complete control of the Organization, but donors are allowed to make recommendations as to their distribution. (Advise and consult funds are reported as designated net assets.)

Endowment Funds

Endowments are established by donors to provide investments with investment earnings to be used for charitable purposes. The Organization also directs the establishment of certain endowment funds of which principal or income may be expended as directed. (Endowments of the Organization are reported as unrestricted designated net assets because principal and income are expendable at the discretion of the board. Endowments are also administered for others.)

Contributed Services and Materials

Contributed services are reported in the financial statements for voluntary donations of services when those services: (1) create or enhance non-financial assets; or (2) require specialized skills provided by individuals possessing those skills and are services that would be typically purchased if not provided by donation.

Donated materials are recorded at their fair value at the date of the gift. The Organization does not imply time restrictions for gifts of long-lived assets. As a result, in the absence of donor-imposed restrictions, gifts of long-lived assets are reported as unrestricted revenue.

....

Note X: Summary of Significant Accounting Policies [*portion of longer note*]

Principles of Consolidation—The accompanying consolidated financial statements include the financial position, changes in net assets, and cash flows of the Ballet and the Foundation because the Ballet has both control and economic interest in the Foundation. Inter-organizational transactions and accounts have been eliminated in the consolidation.

....

Note X: Organization and Accounting Policies

Organization

The American [*Disease*] Society, Inc. (the Society), is the nationwide, community-based, voluntary health organization dedicated to eliminating [*disease*] as a major health problem by preventing [*disease*], saving lives, and diminishing suffering from [*disease*], through education, advocacy, and service.

Principles of Consolidation

The accompanying combined financial statements include the accounts of the National Home Office of the Society (the National Home Office) and the American [*Disease*] Society Foundation (the Foundation), which are [*State*] not-for-profit corporations, and its 58 Chartered Divisions (the Divisions), which are separately incorporated under the laws of the various states, the District of Columbia, and Puerto Rico. All significant intra-Society accounts and transactions have been eliminated in the accompanying combined financial statements.

....

Note X: Summary of Significant Accounting Policies [*portion of longer note*]

Perpetual trusts—The Federation is the beneficiary of perpetual trusts held by other entities, as trustees. The Federation's beneficial interest in these trusts is recorded at the fair market value of the assets underlying the trusts.

Pooled life income fund—The Federation has established a pooled life income fund held by another entity, as trustee. Each donor to the fund shall receive a proportionate share of the fund's income during the donor's lifetime. Upon each donor's death, the units in the fund attributable to that donor shall become the property of the Federation and shall be added to its Endowment Fund. The Federation's beneficial interest in the fund is recorded at the fair market value of the assets underlying the fund.

Note X: Nature of Operations

[*Disease*] Association, Inc. (the Association) is a nonprofit, tax-exempt corporation whose purpose is to fight [*Disease*] on all fronts. The Association's mission is carried out through research into the cause, prevention, treatment and cure; education of the public and information for health care professionals; chapter formation for a nationwide family support network; advocacy for improved public policy and needed legislation; and patient and family services to aid present and future victims and caregivers.

Note X: Nature of Operations and Related Parties

American [*XYZ*] Association (A[*XYZ*]A) is a national, not-for-profit voluntary health agency dedicated to the conquest of [*XYZ*] disease. The Association conducts programs to inform the public of air conservation, occupational health, smoking, and health hazards, [*XYZ*] disease, and community health. It also conducts professional education programs in these same areas, which include the sponsorship of symposia, conferences, and meetings among medical professionals, as well as publications, films, fellowships, and research grants.

Related Parties

There are 59 constituent [*XYZ*] Associations, which have jurisdiction over specific geographic areas or over certain of the 76 affiliated [*XYZ*] Associations. Each constituent and/or affiliated [*XYZ*] Association is required to remit 10% of its shareable income to A[*XYZ*]A. In return, A[*XYZ*]A provides supplies and certain services to its constituents' programs. Supplies provided by A[*XYZ*]A include health education materials, which are provided at a price which approximates cost.

Note X: Basis of Presentation

[*University*] is a private not-for-profit educational institution, organized into seven schools on three campuses, with 1,500 faculty and over 17,000 graduate and undergraduate students.

The financial statements include the accounts of the University. In addition the University manages and operates [*Affiliated Research Laboratory*] for the United States Department of [*XX*] under a management and operating contract; therefore the revenues and expenditures of [*Laboratory*] are included in the statement of activities. [*Affiliated Institution*] is an integral part of the University and is included in the financial statements. Auxiliary activities include Housing and Dining Services, intercollegiate athletics, and certain patient care provided by the School of Medicine.

....

Note X: Basis of Accounting

The accounts of the Organization are maintained on the accrual basis in accordance with the principles of fund accounting. Separate accounts are maintained for each fund; however, the accompanying financial statements have been prepared on a basis which shows the financial position and changes in net assets of the Organization in total. Funds with similar characteristics have been combined for financial statement presentation into the following categories.

- Funds with Unrestricted Net Assets:
  — Operating Fund
  — Board-Designated Funds (including board-designated endowments)
  — Property Fund

- Funds with Temporarily Restricted Net Assets:
  — Research Fund
  — Deferred Gifts Fund
  — Scholarship Fund
  — Term Endowment Funds

- Funds with Permanently Restricted Net Assets:
  — Challenge Endowment Fund
  — Permanent Endowment Funds

....

[*Presented below are examples of two notes used to describe non-GAAP policies with an immaterial effect on the financial statements.*]

Note X: Basis of Accounting [*Financial statements are on a GAAP basis.*]

The Organization does not provide an allowance for uncollectible pledges receivable, but rather expenses such items in the period they become uncollectible. This practice differs from generally accepted accounting principles, but its impact is deemed immaterial.

Note X: Basis of Accounting [*Financial statements are on a GAAP basis.*]

The College recognizes interest and dividend income substantially on the cash basis and does not amortize bond premiums or accrete bond discount, except that the discount on zero-coupon bonds is accreted, and the income on guaranteed investment contracts is accrued. The difference between such policies and that which would result from following the full accrual, amortization, and accretion methods is not material.

....

[*In the "Unrestricted" section of this note, the organization points out that not all the unrestricted net assets are automatically available for general purposes.*]

Note X: Net Asset Categories

Permanently restricted net assets are those that may never be spent by the Organization, including gifts of endowment and for student loan principal, as well as the earnings on those assets when permanently restricted by the donor. Also included in this category are contributions receivable and living trust principal that are permanently restricted upon redemption or maturity, certain museum collection objects which, by donor stipulation, may never be deaccessioned, and undeveloped land which is subject to a perpetual conservation easement prohibiting future commercial use.

Temporarily restricted net assets carry restrictions that expire upon the passage of a prescribed period or upon the occurrence of a stated event as specified by the donor. Included in this category are gifts held by the Organization pending their use in accordance with donor stipulations, unexpended gifts for capital projects, term endowments, and pledges and living trust agreements where the principal is expendable upon redemption or maturity.

Unrestricted net assets, as defined by The Financial Accounting Standards Board (FASB), are composed of all resources not included in the above categories. Included are expendable resources used to support the Organization's core activities of [*description of activities*]. Donor-restricted contributions that are received and expended in the same year are classified as unrestricted. Donor-restricted resources intended for capital projects are released and reclassified as unrestricted support when the related assets are placed in service. All expenses are recorded as a reduction to unrestricted net assets.

However, in reality, a substantial portion of these assets is not available for general Organization purposes. Included in unrestricted net assets are significant resources subject to contractual agreements with external parties. Also included are $350 million in realized and unrealized endowment gains, which have been accumulated under an Organization policy designed to maintain the spending power of the original endowment over time. In addition, approximately $450 million of these net assets are invested in the

Organization's property, plant, and equipment, and in its equity in [*Affiliate*]. While FASB requires that all these resources be reported as unrestricted, the Organization manages them in compliance with Board designations, legal requirements, and contractual obligations.

....

Note X: Endowment

The University endowments include pure endowment, term endowments, funds functioning as endowment, and funds subject to living trust agreements. These resources are recorded as permanently restricted, temporarily restricted, and unrestricted net assets, as described below.

Pure endowment funds are subject to restrictions of the gift instruments requiring that the principal be invested in perpetuity, and the income and an appropriate portion of gains only be spent as provided for under the [*State*] Uniform Management of Institutional Funds Act ([*S*]UMIFA). In the absence of further donor restrictions, the amount of gains that are to be expended in a given year is determined through the endowment payout policy discussed in Note [*number*]. The University classifies the original endowment gift and any gains with donor-imposed permanent restrictions as permanently restricted net assets. The Financial Accounting Standards Board (FASB) has determined that the legal limitations imposed by [*S*]UMIFA on realized and unrealized gains on endowments are not permanent restrictions if the gains may be appropriated for expenditure. Accordingly, the University reports a portion of the expendable reinvested gains as temporarily restricted net assets (when the donor's restriction has not yet been met), and the remainder of the expendable reinvested realized and unrealized gains as unrestricted net assets. Notwithstanding this FASB mandated reporting, the University recognizes, for internal management purposes only, the limitations on expending such gains that are specified in [*S*]UMIFA.

Expendable endowment assets include term endowments and funds functioning as endowments. Term endowments are similar to other endowment funds except that upon the passage of a stated period of time or the occurrence of a particular event, all or part of the principal may be expended. These resources are classified as temporarily restricted net assets. Funds functioning as endowments are unrestricted University resources designated as endowment by the [*Governing Board*] and are invested in the endowment for long-term appreciation and current income. However, these assets remain available and may be spent at the Board's discretion. Funds functioning as endowment are recorded as unrestricted net assets.

Funds subject to living trust agreements represent trusts with living income beneficiaries where the University has a residual interest. These funds are recorded in the University's net asset balances at their fair market value. The discounted present value of any income beneficiary interest is reported as a liability on the statement of financial position. Gifts subject to such agreements are recorded net of the income beneficiary share at the date of gift. Actuarial gains and losses are included in the change in value of split-interest agreements. Resources that are expendable upon maturity are classified as temporarily restricted net assets; all others are classified as permanently restricted net assets.

. . . .

[In this example, the temporary restriction was stipulated by the donor, but the Board has placed an additional designation on the amount by deciding to spend only the income from investment of the gift, but not the gift itself. Presumably, the donor was consulted to ascertain that he or she would not object.]

Note X: Designated Temporarily Restricted Net Assets— Musical Endowment

Through a generous gift of [*Person*], an endowment has been created to assist in the production of musicals at [*Theater*]. The principal will be invested and the earnings of the fund allocated at the discretion of management for support of the production of musicals at [*Theater*]. The decision to maintain the corpus of this fund is not a requirement of the gift, but is the choice of the Board of Trustees and may be changed at its discretion.

CONTINGENCIES AND OTHER UNCERTAINTIES, INCLUDING GOING CONCERN QUESTIONS

Note X: Contingencies

The Organization has guaranteed certain obligations, principally mortgages and leases on properties owned by related parties, totaling $17,200,000 at June 30, 20X2.

Various lawsuits, claims, and other contingent liabilities arise in the ordinary course of the Organization's activities. In December 20X1 a $400,000 settlement, including damages, was reached with the United States Department of Health and Human Services for alleged billing errors totaling approximately $350,000, under Part B of the Medicare Program during the period 20VV-20WW. The effect of the settlement had no material impact on the Statement of Activities for fiscal year 20X2.

Based upon information currently available with respect to the aforementioned contingencies, management believes that any liability resulting therefrom will not materially affect the financial position or operations of the Organization.

. . . .

Note X: Guarantee of Indebtedness

The Organization is a guarantor of mortgage debt of ABC Residence Corp. The principal balance of the loan is $1,263,000 at December 31, 20X2. The total remaining scheduled payments through 20Y6 are $1,897,000. The guarantee arose under the original terms of the loan agreement. Payments by the Organization under the guarantee would occur upon ABC Residence Corp.'s failure to make principal and interest payments when due. The loan is secured by the related real estate. Management of the Organization expects that proceeds from the sale of the mortgaged property would exceed the debt.

. . . .

Note X: Guarantees

In connection with arrangements between the College and ABC Bank, DEF Bank, and GHI Bank, the College guarantees loans taken out by students to pay their current account balance at the College. Total loans guaranteed by the College approximated $281,000 as of June 30, 20X2. The guarantees last over the terms of the respective loans through 20Y2. In the event of default, the College repurchases the loan from the bank and resumes collection efforts with respect to the loan.

. . . .

Note X: Contingencies, Commitments, and Guarantees

The Foundation is involved in several legal actions. The Foundation believes it has defenses for all such claims, believes the claims are substantially without merit, and is vigorously defending the actions. In the opinion of management, the final disposition of these matters will not have a material effect on the Foundation's financial position. The Foundation, as part of its program-related investment activities, has outstanding loan guarantees of $950,000 and is committed to provide $1,953,000 of loans to nonprofit organizations. Further, as part of its investment management activity, the Foundation is committed to additional funding of $9,980,000 in venture capital partnerships and real estate investment trusts.

. . . .

Note X: Contingencies and Commitments

A claim has been filed in the amount of $10,000,000 in connection with injuries allegedly sustained by a performer who appeared in a [*Performing Arts Center*] production in December 20X1. If and to the extent that the Center is liable, management and counsel believe that the Center will not incur a loss because any claim will be paid by [*City*] and/or pursuant to insurance coverage with limits adequate to cover the claim as thus far asserted.

The Center has entered into commitments related to performances, conductors, guest artists, and certain employees regarding payments for service through fiscal year 20X3 in the amount of $2,373,841.

As of September 29, 20X2, approximately 40% of the Center's employees are members of various labor unions. These labor unions are for Box Office, Stagehands, Wardrobe, and Musicians. During fiscal year 20X2, all union agreements terminated, except for Musicians which terminates on September 1, 20X3. As of November 27, 20X2, the Center renegotiated all of the union agreements, except for the Box Office. The new union contracts included inflationary salary increases for each year negotiated.

Delays in agreeing on labor contracts when they expire could result in work stoppage and the cancellation of Center performances and a loss of revenues.

The Musicians union agreement was negotiated in September 20W9. As part of this renegotiated agreement, the musicians are to receive increasing salary raises through fiscal year 20X3, which will average approximately 14% for the year. This increase will increase [*Orchestra*] program costs by more than $1 million, and it is not likely that such costs will be recovered through operating revenues. Therefore, if the Musicians agreement is not modified, the Center will need to generate additional revenues or reduce costs of programs to offset the expected increased cost of orchestra programs.

The [*Orchestra*] has incurred losses for several years. The ability of the Center to continue to reduce and eliminate its operating deficit is dependent on, among other things, the ability of management to reduce the losses incurred by the orchestra.

....

Note X: Uncertainties

[*Project*] of the Organization has been funded by the United States Agency for International Development (USAID) grants and contracts. However, the Organization used a portion of the amounts advanced from USAID to finance its match portion of the project and to finance general operations. At year end, the Organization is obligated to complete approximately $148,000 of federal and counterpart commitments on this project and, additionally, may be liable for disallowed costs, as referred to in Note [*number*]. In addition, the Organization has borrowed $125,000 from endowment investments to pay operating expenses, is delinquent in paying short-term obligations, and is liable on an outstanding line of credit of $125,000 at December 31, 20X2. These conditions create an uncertainty about the Organization's ability to continue as a going concern. Management of the Organization plans to reach an agreement with USAID regarding the above issues and continue to meet short-term obligations by receiving contributions from its Board of Directors and through program revenues. The financial statements do not include any adjustments that might be necessary if the Organization is unable to continue as a going concern.

....

Note X: Risks and Uncertainties

The Organization is engaged primarily in training hard-core unemployed persons to re-enter the job market. Funding for its programs is from the U.S. Department of Labor (80%) and private foundation grants (20%). The Organization is paid by the U.S. Department of Labor based upon the number of persons successfully trained. Certain persons may not complete the training program and, thus, the Organization will not be paid for the training of those persons.

. . . .

Note X: Union Contract

Most non-management personnel of the Organization are members of the XYZ Union. The collective bargaining agreement will terminate in April 20X3. Negotiations between management and the Union have commenced. It is not possible at this time to determine what the financial impact of a new contract will be on the Organization.

. . . .

Note X: Government Support

The Organization received a substantial amount of its operating support from state and local governments. Any significant reduction in the level of this support could have an effect on the Organization's programs.

. . . .

Note X: Contingent Liabilities

The Organization has not fully complied with certain requirements applicable to its financial awards program. Consequently, some costs may subsequently be disallowed by the affected funding agency. The amount of costs which may subsequently be disallowed, if any, cannot be reasonably estimated.

. . . .

Note X: Commitments and Contingencies

The University conducts substantial sponsored research for the federal government pursuant to contracts and grants from federal agencies and departments. The [*Federal Department*] is the cognizant federal agency for determining indirect cost rates charged to federally sponsored agreements.

During 20W8, disagreements arose between the University and [*Department*] over the appropriateness of some of the University's indirect and similar charges, as well as the methods used to allocate specific indirect costs to those agreements. In June 20X1, the University settled its contractual disputes with the federal government and agreed to pay $565,000 and dismiss its claims for underrecovery.

The University is still defending an action alleging inappropriate allocations and billings of indirect costs for earlier years. The University believes it has meritorious defenses and intends vigorously to contest any such claims or litigation. The University believes that resolution of this suit will not have a material adverse effect on its financial position.

The University has substantially settled overhead rates applicable to 20X1 and prior years on government contracts. Project revenue for 20X2 includes an amount for overhead applicable to billings to the United States Government which is subject to possible increase or decrease by negotiation. In the opinion of management, adequate provision has been made in the accounts for any adjustment that may result.

· ·

Note X: Facilities Renovations and Earthquake Damage

As a result of changes in federal regulations, state building codes, and a major earthquake in 20W9, the University has committed to make seismic improvements, code upgrades, and repairs to campus buildings. The University estimates that approximately $25,600,000 of repairs and upgrades remains to be made. A number of campus buildings suffered structural damage in the earthquake which forced their closure. In connection with state and local legislation, the University has submitted a plan to [County] to strengthen certain buildings by September 20X4. The University has determined that certain other (nonseismic) improvements, while technically required only for new construction, are important to conform campus buildings to the current Uniform Building Code.

As of June 30, 20X2, the Federal Emergency Management Agency has reimbursed $16,000,000 to the University and has agreed to fund an additional $7,300,000. The University plans to finance the remaining costs with gifts, debt, and other existing funds.

· ·

Note X: Litigation Matters

In August 20X2, the [City] Police Department arrested a long-time employee of the Organization on charges of felony theft. The employee was allegedly stealing from the Organization box office cash receipts. Related to this matter, the Organization filed an insurance claim and a lawsuit against the former employee; the arrested employee filed a counterclaim asserting wrongful termination and defamation. On August 26, 20X2, trial in this matter was concluded and the Organization prevailed in its claim for wrongful conversion of funds. The Court awarded the Organization damages of $172,555 plus costs, which, because of the uncertainty of collection, has not been reflected in the financial statements as of June 30, 20X2.

· ·

[*FASB Statement No. 5*, Accounting for Contingencies, *sets a very high standard to be met before a contingent asset may be recorded. However, note disclosure of such matters is appropriate.*]

Note X: Unrecorded Contributions

During fiscal year 20X1, the School was notified that it had been bequeathed a portion of the estate of a deceased donor. As of July 31, 20X2, the amount to be received by the School was indeterminable pending finalization of certain legal and estate tax matters.

During fiscal year 20X1, the School, as co-recipient with three other nonprofit organizations, received an unrestricted donation of approximately 120 acres of unimproved real estate in a neighboring county. The property is being held for sale with the net proceeds to be divided equally among the recipients, but the amount which may ultimately be realized is not presently determinable.

In view of the uncertainty of the ultimate amounts to be received, the School has not recognized the foregoing contributions. Accordingly, the financial statements will not reflect these amounts until such time as they are received in the form of cash, or until the actual amounts to be received can be determined with reasonable certainty.

. . . .

Note X: Federal Income Tax [*See also other tax-related notes in Chapter 7.*]

The Organization is a nonprofit corporation that paid Federal income tax at prevailing corporate rates on its unrelated business taxable income for years prior to 20W9. As a result of uncertainties as to its obligations to pay Federal income tax, no payments have been made for years from 20W9 through 20X1, and a payment of $150,000 was made for 20X2. At December 31, 20X2, provision has been made for additional Federal income tax which may be payable for years from 20W9 through 20X2 in the aggregate amount of $1,200,000, including accrued interest of $135,000.

In 20X2, an Internal Revenue Service agent completed examination of the Organization's tax returns for the years 20W9 through 20X1 and proposed revocation of the Organization's exempt status commencing in 20W9. Should the agent's proposal ultimately be upheld, the Organization's liability for income taxes and interest would be approximately $3,500,000 more than the amount accrued at December 31, 20X2. The Organization has protested the agent's findings, and, in the opinion of the Organization's management and legal counsel, the findings are without merit.

. . . .

Note X: Real Estate Taxes

On May 1, 20X1, the town of [*Town*], where the arboretum facility of the [*Botanical Garden*] is located, revoked the real property tax exemption for that property effective fiscal 20X2. The Board of Assessment Review upheld the action of the Assessor on July 20, 20X1. The Garden has filed petitions in the Supreme Court of [*State*] to overturn this decision. Although the outcome of this litigation may not be predicted with certainty, it is the opinion of counsel that said property should be exempt from real estate taxation. If upheld, the action of the Assessor will result in real estate taxes owed the town of [*Town*] in the amount of approximately $115,000 for the fiscal year ending June 30, 20X3. A similar amount was accrued and paid under protest during the fiscal year ended June 30, 20X2.

. . . .

Note X: Management's Plans

In 20X1, the Organization began the renovation of the [*Theatre*]. Final costs were approximately $20 million, which was greater than the original budgeted costs. In addition, the Organization suffered revenue losses due to the closure of the [*Theatre*] during the renovation. The [*Theatre*] was reopened in January 20X2.

As of June 30, 20X2, the Organization has negative net assets of $604,905. This is directly attributable to the renovation of the [*Theatre*], including the loan discussed in Note [*number*]. Because the organization has no long-term assurance of continuing use of the [*Theatre*], the renovation costs are not considered an asset of the Organization (see Note [*number*]).

[*Note: This treatment is unusual; generally, leasehold improvements are reflected as an asset.*]

The management of the Organization anticipates eliminating the negative net asset balance through a combination of the following activities:

- The Organization is a plaintiff in a lawsuit and management expects to prevail and obtain damages.
- Management anticipates an increase of revenues from the Facility Free Ticket Surcharge as a result of increased ticket sales for various performances at the [*Music Center*] complex, particularly the [*Theatre*] season.
- Management has reduced staff and instituted a freeze on spending, except for budgeted projects.
- The Organization's sublease with the [*County*] contains a provision that for any fiscal year where expenses exceed revenues, the Organization can submit a bill to the [*County*] for the deficit which shall be paid by the County within 60 days.

. . . .

Note X: Bonds Payable

Principal payments of $113,703 on the dormitory bonds with the Department of Housing and Urban Development (HUD) have not been paid when due during fiscal 20X2 and prior years; in addition, interest payments of $17,755 have not been paid when due during such years. During fiscal 20X2, interest payments of $44,949 were made; $34,325 was applied to delinquent interest and the remainder to fiscal 20X2 interest. The nonpayment of principal and interest constitutes an event of default under the indentures relating to the bonds and enables the Trustees to declare the remaining balance immediately due and payable; the Trustees have not taken such action. Officials of the College have been negotiating with HUD to obtain deferments and/or moratorium on the required deposits and principal and interest payments. The College's administration expects to make payments in fiscal 20X3 which will liquidate the delinquent interest amounts and begin reducing the delinquent principal balances.

The dormitory bond indentures with HUD contain provisions which require that net revenues of [*Dormitory*] and the North Campus cafeteria, or certain minimum amounts, whichever is greater, be deposited with a trustee. The College has not made such deposits and the unrestricted net assets balance was reduced in prior years to reflect the deposit obligation amounting to $136,910.

The library building bond indenture with HUD contains provisions which require the College to maintain debt service deposits with a trustee in the amount of $23,000. The College has been granted an indefinite moratorium, which may be terminated upon 30 days notice, on the requirement to maintain such deposit until the principal and interest delinquencies have been paid.

RELATED PARTIES

GENERAL MATTERS

Not-for-profit organizations are often related to other organizations in various ways. One organization may carry out program, management, or fund-raising activities on behalf of another, or two or more organizations may conduct joint program or fund-raising activities, share staff or facilities, or operate under an affiliation agreement with a national organizational parent such as a charity, religious denomination, or association. Organizations may also be considered related parties to organizations with which their officers, directors, trustees, key employees, or major donors are otherwise affiliated.

Note X: Principles of Combination

The financial statements report the worldwide ministries of [*Organization*] International including material liabilities, net assets, revenues, and expenses of its 27 fields of service around the world. The statements do not include the assets, liabilities, net assets, revenues, and expenses of [*Organization*]-Canada not held by or remitted to [*Organization*] International under the joint-ministries agreement because [*Organization*]-Canada is not controlled by either

[*Organization*]-U.S. or [*Organization*] International. As a participant in the joint-ministries agreement, [*Organization*]-Canada provided contributions of $1,369,765 and $1,543,120 (in U.S. dollars) to [*Organization*] International during 20X2 and 20X1, respectively. The statements include all international and U.S. operations which are conducted under the joint-ministries agreement and all contributions from [*Organization*]-Canada for specific projects and missionary support accounts.

[*Organization*]-Canada is audited by other auditors who reported on financial statements which disclosed the following:

| | December 31, | |
	20X2	20X1
	(in Canadian dollars)	
Total assets	1,158,578	1,069,100
Total liabilities	52,857	66,021
Total net assets	1,105,721	1,003,079
Total revenues	3,255,957	3,228,004
Total expenses	3,083,138	3,202,900

Note X: Changes in Affiliation

Changes in the composition of the Affiliates included in the combined financial statements occur for several reasons:

* New organizations are affiliated with the Foundation; or

* Organizations cease to be affiliated with the Foundation; or,

* Organizations fail to comply with the affiliation agreement, including financial reporting requirements. Such organizations are included in the combined financial statements of subsequent years, if compliance with the financial reporting requirements is met.

For Affiliates that have net assets as of the beginning of the year of change in affiliation, such changes are accounted for in the combined financial statements as though they took place as of the beginning of such year.

The following summarizes the changes in net assets for the year ended December 31, 20X2:

Additions resulting from financial reports submitted in the current year but not in the prior year	$1,700,822
Reductions resulting from financial reports not submitted in the current year but which were in the prior year	(8,435)
	$1,692,387

Note X: Related-Party Transactions

An officer of the Foundation is also a director or partner of two organizations, both of which lease space from the Foundation. The Foundation earned approximately $385,700 of sublease income pursuant to these arrangements in 20X2.

During 20X2, the Foundation entered into an agreement with [*Other Organization*] Program, Inc. (OOP), a separate 501(c)(3) exempt organization. Certain board members of OOP are currently trustees of the Foundation. OOP agreed to transfer operating assets and liabilities of $388,267 and $26,319, respectively, at June 30, 20X2, and future contributions and investment income earned on its endowment funds (which had a market value of approximately $575,000 at June 30, 20X2) to the Foundation. The financial statements do not reflect future amounts to be earned on OOP's endowment fund and future contributions for operations, which are not presently determinable.

....

Note X: Related-Party Transactions

The [*Organization*] is affiliated with numerous agencies of the [*Denomination*] Church, including dioceses, parishes, welfare agencies, committees, schools, and missions. Related-party transactions and balances include:

	Years Ended December 31,	
	20X2	*20X1*
Support and expenses:		
Support from committees and agencies	$ 218,149	$ 229,556
Contributions to committees and agencies, ministries, and churches:		
Unrestricted distributions	1,314,931	1,076,812
Distributions of funds held for others	271,912	612,318
Rent expense paid to administrative committee	21,600	20,883
Assets and liabilities:		
Due from committees and agencies	$ 24,171	$ 23,534

....

Note X: [*Organization*] Foundation, Inc.

In 20X1, the Board of Directors of the Organization formed the Foundation for the purpose of holding certain investments and soliciting contributions on behalf of the Organization. The Foundation Board of Directors includes certain directors of the Organization, and its bylaws require that all contributions and earnings on invested assets inure to the benefit of the Organization. Accordingly, the accounts of the Foundation have been consolidated herein, as required by generally accepted accounting procedures.

....

Note X: [*Organization*] Foundation

The [*Organization*] Foundation is an independent corporation formed for the purpose of obtaining and disbursing funds for the sole benefit of the Organization, although the elements of control necessary for consolidation are not present. The September 30, 20X2, unaudited financial statements of the Foundation reflect assets and corresponding net assets of $17,780,000. Assets consist primarily of cash and investments. Revenues for the year ended September 30, 20X2, principally gifts, approximated $11,300,000. Expenditures and transfers to the Organization approximated $1,100,000 and $4,000,000 respectively for the same period.

[*Since the Organization and the Foundation are financially interrelated organizations, as discussed in FASB Statement No. 136,* Transfers of Assets to a Not-for-Profit Organization or Charitable Trust That Raises or Holds Contributions for Others, *the Organization would normally record its interest in the net assets of the Foundation as an asset.*]

••••••••••••••••••••••••

Note X: [*Related Organization*]

Effective January 1, 20X2, the Organization's Board of Directors agreed to a merger with [*Related Organization, Inc.*] (RO), a not-for-profit organization which serves vision-impaired individuals in central [*State*]. The merger was accounted for similar to a pooling of interests. Accordingly, the Organization's consolidated financial statements have been restated to include the results of [*RO*] for all periods presented.

Combined and separate results of [*Organization*] and [*RO*] during the year ended September 30, 20X2 and the three months ended December 31, 2002 were as follows:

	Organization	RO	Combined
Three months ended December 31, 20X2:			
Revenues	$1,704,071	$ 6,937	$1,711,008
Change in net assets	334,693	(21,141)	313,552
Year ended September 30, 20X2:			
Revenues	5,624,942	106,456	5,731,398
Change in net assets	523,364	(13,226)	510,138

••••••••••••••••••••••••

Note X: Intercorporate Agreement

An intercorporate agreement between [*College*] and [*University*] provides for payment for the exchange of certain services between the two institutions. These services include cross-registration for students, library services, faculty exchange, and certain special services and support costs. During the year ended June 30, 20X2, [*College*] paid [*University*] $1,540,000 for services provided under the terms of the agreement.

....

Note X: Related Parties

The facilities occupied by the School are owned by the Sisters of the [*Religious Order*] (Monastery). The School has an agreement with the Monastery to lease the facilities at a rental rate based upon area occupied. The Monastery assumes all the costs for payments on the Monastery's building loan, insurance, additions, and improvements to the physical plant. The costs of operating and maintaining the physical plant are apportioned between the Monastery and the School.

....

Note X: Conflict-of-Interest Policy

It is the policy of the Association that all Officers, Directors, and Committee members shall avoid any conflict between their own individual interests and the interests of the Association. Included among the Association's Board members and officers are volunteers from the financial, medical, and scientific community who provide valuable assistance to the Association in the development of policies and programs, and in evaluating awards and grants. The Association has a conflict-of-interest policy whereby board and committee members must advise the board of any direct or indirect interest in any transaction or relationship with the Association and not participate in discussions and decisions regarding any action affecting their individual, professional, or business interests.

....

Note X: Agreement With [*City*]

Master Agreement—the building and land in which the [*Center*] (Center) is located, is owned by [*City*] (City) and leased to the Organization. Thus the building and underlying land are not assets of the Organization and are not reflected in the financial statements. The Organization operates the Center under a year-to-year lease with the City. As part of this agreement, the Organization is to make available to the City, without charge, the premises up to three times per calendar year.

Under the agreement, in place of cash rent for the use of the premises, the consideration to the City from the Organization will be the continuous operation, development, and maintenance of the premises. The only additional consideration is the one-time payment to the City of the difference between the amount remaining to retire the original construction bonds and the amount in the [*Authority*] Reserve of $46,591. This amount, which was included in accrued expenses at June 30, 20X2, was paid in July 20X2.

[*Note: If the cost of continuous operation, development, and maintenance of the premises is materially less than the fair rental value of the premises, the Organization would need to recognize the additional amount up to fair rental value as revenue and expense.*]

....

Note X: Related-Party Transactions

During the year ended March 31, 20X2, the Organization paid $48,000 for legal services provided by a firm, one of the partners of which is the Organization's president and a member of the [*Governing Board*]. In addition, the Organization has notes receivable of $34,000 from [*Debtor*], nephew of [*Board Member*], chairperson of the [*Governing Board*].

....

Note X: Related Parties

Grants were awarded to the [*Other not-for-profit organization*] of $20,582,000 in 20X2 and $18,130,000 in 20X1. Certain directors of the Foundation are also directors of this organization. Directors of the Foundation are not permitted to vote on proposed grants to organizations for which they serve as officers or directors.

MERGERS AND SPINOFFS

See Accounting Principles Board (APB) Opinion Nos. 16, *Business Combinations*, and 20, *Accounting Changes*, for additional guidance; see also paragraphs 1.15 through 1.16 of the AICPA Audit and Accounting Guide *Not-for-Profit Organizations* for comment on use of the pooling method by not-for-profits. In addition, the FASB currently has a project underway to develop guidance on the accounting and reporting for combinations of not-for-profit organizations. As this publication goes to press, it appears that the pooling method will not be permitted in the future. Merging not-for-profit organizations will be required to apply purchase accounting.

Note X: Change in Reporting Entity [*Two-year report; August 31 year end*]

The financial statement presentation of the [*Organization*] was changed in 20X2 to include the accounts of [*Affiliate*]. The 20X1 financial statements have been restated to reflect this change. The restatement increased the previously reported net assets as of September 1, 20X0 and 20X1 by $1,433,958 and $1,502,774, respectively, and decreased the previously reported 20X1 excess of revenues over expenses by $68,235.

....

Note X: Merger [*Two-year report; December 31 year end*]

On November 8, 20X2, a merger of [*Organization*] and [*Merged Organization*] was consummated by votes of the respective boards of directors. The merger was accounted for as a "pooling of interests." The accompanying financial statements reflect the combined assets, liabilities, and net assets of the two organizations at December 31, 20X2, and the support, revenue, expenses, and changes in net assets, and functional expenses for the entire year 20X2. The effect of the merger on net assets and on the change in net assets for 20X2 and as previously reported for 20X1 was:

	20X2	20X1
Net assets, beginning of year, as previously reported	$ 1,756	$ 1,556
Adjustment for effect of merger	224	213
Net assets, as restated	1,980	1,769
Change in net assets for the year—increase (decrease)	32	(47)

· ·

Note X: Spinoff of Affiliate [*One-year report; June 30, 20X2 year end*]

The Board of Trustees of [*Organization*] adopted a resolution on April 22, 20X0 authorizing the [*Affiliated Organization*] to pursue a plan for separate incorporation. [*Affiliate*] was officially incorporated as a separate entity to begin operations on July 1, 20X1. The separate incorporation led to the transfer after June 30, 20X1 of all the assets that the [*Organization*] held for the use of the [*Affiliate*]. These assets had a net book value of $7,300,762.

[*The financial statements for the year 20X2 showed no amounts related to the Affiliate since, under APB Opinion No. 20, the opening net assets balance was restated for the effect of the change in reporting entity.*]

SUMMARIZED FINANCIAL DATA FOR A COMPONENT OF THE ORGANIZATION

Note X: [*University*] Health System—Health Services Component

The University Trustees formed the [*University*] Health Systems in June 20W8. The Health System operates an integrated system which delivers education, research, and patient care. The Health Services Component comprises the Hospital of the [*University*], Clinical Practices of the [*University*], Clinical Care Associates, [*Physician Services, Inc.*] and [*Medical Center of the University*] Health System, which was created as a result of the merger on July 1, 20X1. The [*University*] Health Systems and the Health Services Component are included in the financial statements of the University.

Throughout the year, certain transactions are conducted between the Health Services Component and the University. The effect of these transactions (primarily inter-entity billings for allocations of common costs and certain purchased services) is included in the financial information of the Health Services Component.

The Health Services Component makes transfers from their operations that further the research and educational activities of the School of Medicine. These activities are integral to the overall mission of the Health System and the effect of the transfers is reflected in the Health Services Corporation net assets.

Summarized financial information for the Health Services Component as of June 30, 20X2, prior to elimination for transactions between the Health Services Component and other entities of the University, is as follows:

Net patient service revenue	$ 917,535
Other revenues	52,636
Total expenses	(942,850)
Excess of revenues over expenses from operations	27,321
Nonoperating gains, net	47,987
Excess of revenues over expenses	$ 75,308
Total current assets	327,262
Investments and assets whose use is limited (including board-designated funds of $464,618 and trustee-held funds of $172,576)	793,923
Property, plant, and equipment, net	533,015
Other assets	93,219
Total assets	$1,747,419
Total current liabilities	$238,302
Long-term debt, net of current portion	651,405
Other liabilities	276,420
Total liabilities	1,166,127
Net assets	
Unrestricted	466,760
Temporarily restricted	81,562
Permanently restricted	32,970
Total net assets	581,292
Total liabilities and net assets	$1,747,419

· ·

Note X: Blood Services Component—Unrestricted, Designated Net Assets

The following is a summary of unrestricted operations and changes in net assets of the Blood Services component of the organization for the years ended June 30, 20X2 and 20X1, including the operations and changes in net assets of the regional blood services and national sector.

| | For the Year Ended June 30, | |
	20X2	*20X1*
Revenues		
Blood Services processing	$600,878	$518,084
Investment income	5,491	5,686
Other income	20,313	11,777
Total revenues	626,682	535,547
Expenses		
Blood Services	618,144	531,592
Excess of revenues over expenses before property and equipment transactions	8,538	3,955
Loss from sales of property	(26,229)	(24,645)
Change in Net Assets, applied to:		
Decrease in designated balances approved by board action for:		
Replacement and improvement of buildings and equipment	$(3,954)	
Other specific purposes	(9,559)	
Net operating assets available for remaining operations	(4,178)	(17,691) (20,690)
Net Assets, beginning of year		188,424 209,114
Net Assets, end of year		$170,733 $188,424

The following is a statement of Blood Services unrestricted net assets at June 30, 20X2 and 20X1 including the financial position of the regional blood services and national sector.

| | June 30 | |
	20X2	*20X1*
Assets		
Cash and time deposits	$ 10,504	$ 11,836
Investments	59,195	80,141
Receivables	89,957	69,516
Inventories	85,071	77,031
Other assets	3,364	2,326
Total assets	248,091	240,850
Liabilities		
Accounts payable and accrued liabilities	45,510	38,247
Notes payable	1,180	9,272
Due to unconsolidated affiliates	30,668	4,907
Total liabilities	77,358	52,426
Net Assets	$170,733	$188,424

	June 30	
	20X2	*20X1*
Net assets—as designated:		
Replacement and improvements of buildings and equipment	$ 23,576	$ 27,530
Other specific purposes	37,699	47,258
Net assets required for operations	109,458	113,636
Net Assets as above	$170,733	$188,424

USE OF ESTIMATES

See SOP 94-6, *Disclosure of Certain Significant Risks and Uncertainties*, for further guidance.

Note X: Use of Estimates in the Preparation of Financial Statements

The preparation of financial statements in conformity with generally accepted accounting principles requires management to make estimates and assumptions that affect the reported amounts of assets and liabilities; the disclosure of contingent assets and liabilities at the date of the financial statements; and the reported amounts of revenues and expenses during the relevant period. Actual results could differ from the estimates.

At June 30, 20X2, reserves had been established for uncollectible accounts, student loans, and contributions receivable. These reserves were estimated based on historical collection and allowance practices as well as on management's evaluation of current trends. The reserves for self-insurance and postretirement medical and life insurance benefits were based on actuarial studies. The University believes that the methods and assumptions used in computing these liabilities are appropriate.

COMPARATIVE PRIOR-PERIOD INFORMATION

See paragraphs 3.20 through 3.21 of the AICPA Audit and Accounting Guide *Not-for-Profit Organizations* for further guidance.

Note X: Prior-Period Information

The financial statements include certain prior-year summarized comparative information in total but not by net asset class. Such information does not include sufficient detail to constitute a presentation in conformity with generally accepted accounting principles. Accordingly, such information should be read in conjunction with the [*Organization's*] financial statements for the year ended June 30, 20X1, from which the summarized information was derived.

Certain prior-year amounts have been reclassified to conform to the current year's financial statement presentation.

FOREIGN OPERATIONS

See also FASB Statement No. 52, *Foreign Currency Translation*, for further guidance.

Note X: Foreign Currency Translation

Substantially all assets and liabilities of the Venice operations are translated at year-end exchange rates; support, revenues, and expenses are translated at the average exchange rates during the year. Translation adjustments for such assets and liabilities are accumulated separately in unrestricted net assets and the accumulated unrealized loss was $57,514 as of December 31, 20X2 (included with unrestricted operating net assets). Gains and losses from foreign currency translation for the period are included in the statement of activities.

....

Note X: Foreign Operations

In connection with its worldwide ministry, RWT maintains facilities in various countries outside the United States. As of December 31, 20X2 and 20X1, respectively, current assets in other countries, including cash, securities, receivables, prepaid expenses, and inventories, totaled $2,323,787 and $1,947,363; property and equipment, net of accumulated depreciation, amounted to $5,752,089 and $5,372,692, and liabilities in other countries were $2,961,904 and $2,476,411. Total overseas support and revenues received from foreign sources amounted to $8,385,524 and $8,958,820 for the years ended December 31, 20X2 and 20X1, respectively.

Account balances relating to foreign operations are reflected in the financial statements in United States dollars.

ACCOUNTING CHANGES

Additional guidance on this subject is in APB Opinion No. 20. Accounting changes made prospectively are reported in the statement of activities for the year of the change. An example of this presentation is in the sample statement of activity for The [*Disease*] Association in Chapter 2 of this publication.

Accounting changes made retroactively require restatement of certain beginning-of-the-year amounts and, if comparative prior-period statements are presented, prior-year amounts. The reconciliation of these amounts as previously reported may be shown either on the face of the statement of activity, or in a note. An example of such a note follows.

Observe that this note is taken from an organization which presents a one-year single-column statement of activity, showing the change in net assets by class, but only total net assets as of the beginning of the prior year. If the statement of activity were comparative, then the net asset number to be restated would be the beginning of the prior year (January 1, 20X1) amount.

Note X: Change in Accounting

In 20X2 the [*Organization*] changed its method of accounting for [*item or transaction*] to adopt the provisions of [*newly-issued FASB Statement No. XXX*]. [*Describe new method of accounting.*]

This change resulted in the following restatement of the 20X1 financial statements:

	[Balance Sheet Item]	Change in Unrestricted Net Assets	Ending Unrestricted Net Assets
December 31, 20X1, balances, as previously reported	$ 766,808	($ 946,487)	$2,071,516
Effect of change in accounting for	(580,286)	37,441	580,286
Balances as restated	$186,522	($ 909,046)	$2,651,802

SAMPLE MANAGEMENT STATEMENT OF RESPONSIBILITY

MANAGEMENT RESPONSIBILITY FOR FINANCIAL STATEMENTS

Statements of responsibility are not technically part of the financial statements themselves. However, when presented they accompany and refer to the statements. An example is included below.

Management Responsibility for Financial Statements

The financial statements on the [*accompanying*] pages have been prepared in conformity with generally accepted accounting principles applicable to [*type of organization*]. The management of [*Organization*] is responsible for the integrity and objectivity of these financial statements.

In accumulating and controlling its financial data, management maintains a highly developed system of internal accounting controls. Management believes that a high level of internal control is maintained by the establishment and communication of accounting and business policies, by the selection and training of qualified personnel, and by a program of internal audits to give it reasonable assurance at reasonable cost that the Organization's assets are protected and that transactions and events are recorded properly.

The accompanying financial statements, where indicated, have been audited by the Organization's independent accountants, [*Firm*]. Their report expresses an informed judgment as to whether management's financial statements considered in their entirety, present fairly, in conformity with generally accepted accounting principles, the Organization's financial position, changes in net assets, and cash flows. The independent accountants' opinion is based on audit procedures described in their report, which include obtaining an understanding of Organization systems, procedures, and internal accounting controls, and performing tests and other auditing procedures to provide reasonable assurance that the financial statements neither are materially misleading nor contain material errors. While the independent accountants make extensive tests of Organization procedures and controls, it is neither practicable nor necessary for them to scrutinize large portions of the Organization's transactions.

The [*Governing Board*], through its Audit Committee composed of members not employed by the Organization, is responsible for engaging the independent accountants and meeting with management, internal auditors, and the independent accountants to assure that each is carrying out its responsibilities, and to discuss auditing, internal control, and financial reporting matters. Both the internal auditors and the independent accountants have full and free access to the Audit Committee. Both meet with the Audit Committee at least annually, with and without each other, and with and without the presence of management representatives.

[*Signed*]

_____   _____
[*Vice President for Financial Affairs*]   [*Controller*]

"SARBANES-OXLEY" PUBLIC ATTESTATION BY ORGANIZATION CEO AND CFO

Although not-for-profit organizations are not covered by the Sarbanes-Oxley Act, they may wish to make the same kind of public attestation about the financial statements and internal controls that is required of public companies. Following is some sample language that could be used (adapted from the SEC certification form for public companies).

CERTIFICATION

I, [*identify the certifying individual*], certify that:

1. Based on my knowledge, the financial statements, and other financial information included in this report, fairly present in all material respects the financial position, changes in net assets, and cash flows of [*Organization*] as of, and for, the periods presented in this report;

2. The organization's other certifying officer(s) and I are responsible for establishing and maintaining internal accounting controls and procedures and internal control over financial reporting and have:

(a) Designed such controls and procedures, or caused such disclosure controls and procedures to be designed under our supervision, to ensure that material information relating to the organization, including its consolidated affiliates, is made known to us by others within those entities, particularly during the period in which this report is being prepared;

(b) Designed such internal control over financial reporting, or caused such internal control over financial reporting to be designed under our supervision, to provide reasonable assurance regarding the reliability of financial reporting and the preparation of financial statements for external purposes in accordance with generally accepted accounting principles [*or other basis, if used*];

(c) Evaluated the effectiveness of the organization's controls and procedures and presented in this report our conclusions about the effectiveness of the controls and procedures, as of a date within 90 days prior to the date of this report based on such evaluation; and

(d) Disclosed in this report any change in the organization's internal control over financial reporting that occurred during the organization's most recent fiscal year that has materially affected, or is reasonably likely to materially affect, the organization's internal control over financial reporting; and

3. The organization's other certifying officer(s) and I have disclosed to the organization's auditors and [*if there is an audit committee*] the audit committee of the organization's board of directors (or persons performing the equivalent functions):

(a) All significant deficiencies and material weaknesses in the design or operation of internal control over financial reporting which are reasonably likely to adversely affect the organization's ability to record, process, summarize, and report financial information; and

(b) Any fraud, whether or not material, that involves management or other employees who have a significant role in the organization's internal control over financial reporting.

Date:_____

_____
[*Signature*]   [*Title*]

In addition, management may wish to include in the notes to the financial statements, language similar to the following:

Note X: Organization and Accounting Policy [*portion of longer note*]

The Organization maintains a system of internal controls designed to provide reasonable assurance that transactions are executed in accordance with management's general or specific authorization; transactions are recorded as necessary (1) to permit preparation of financial statements in conformity with generally accepted accounting principles [*or other basis, if used*], and (2) to maintain accountability for assets; access to assets is permitted only in accordance with management's general or specific authorization; and the recorded accountability for assets is compared with the existing assets at reasonable intervals and appropriate action is taken with respect to any differences.

CHAPTER 6: Sample Disclosures Related Primarily to the Statement of Financial Position

Note that these sample notes are not necessarily complete for any given organization's circumstances.

See also Chapter 7 for notes describing revenue and expense amounts, many of which have balance sheet effects.

INVESTMENTS

See paragraph 11 of Financial Accounting Standards Board (FASB) Statement of Financial Accounting Standards No. 124, *Accounting for Certain Investments Held by Not-for-Profit Organizations*, and paragraph 8.33 of the AICPA Audit and Accounting Guide *Not-for-Profit Organizations* (the Guide) for a discussion of investment gains. Note that individual state laws should also be consulted.

Note X: Investments

Investments are generally recorded at fair value based upon quoted market prices, when available, or estimates of fair value. Donated assets are recorded at fair value at the date of donation, or, if sold immediately after receipt, at the amount of sales proceeds received (which are considered a fair measure of the value at the date of donation). Those investments for which fair value is not readily determinable are carried at cost or, if donated, at fair value at the date of donation, or, if no value can be estimated, at a nominal value. The fair value of donated developed real estate is estimated based on discounted cash flows of existing leases. The Organization records the change of ownership of bonds and stocks on the day a trade is made.

Endowment Payout/Spending Rule. The Organization uses a total-return concept in determining allowable spending for endowment and quasi-endowment funds invested in the Long-Term Balanced Pool. The spending rule is that in each fiscal year, an amount between 3.5% and 6% of the market value of the pool (measured on a three-year moving average) be allocated to holders of units of the pool. The amount should equal the amount allocated in the previous fiscal year, adjusted by the net change in the projected Consumer Price Index. If endowment income received is not sufficient to support the total-return objective, the balance is provided from realized and unrealized gains. If income received is in excess of the objective, the balance is reinvested in the Long-Term Balanced Pool on behalf of the unit holders. The other investment pools have a policy of allocating current income.

Investment Market Value. The following chart shows investments held by the Organization as of June 30, 20X2.

	Cost	Estimated Fair Value
Equity securities		
Domestic	$ 598,692	$631,982
International	261,529	265,808
Debt securities		
Domestic—government	349,598	339,774
Domestic—corporate debt securities	167,890	165,290
Domestic—mortgage-backed securities	12,154	11,712
International	35,349	49,843
Other investments		
Distressed securities	35,677	40,692
Hedge funds	70,000	90,666
Oil and gas	4,626	3,769
Private equity	37,087	42,520
Real estate	93,552	109,457
Other	63,596	65,462
Total investments	$1,729,750	$1,816,975

Investment Return. The components of total investment return as of June 30, 20X2, were as follows:

Investment income	$ 91,035
Net realized gains	323,701
Net change in unrealized gains on investments reported at fair value	(197,030)
Total investment return	$ 217,706

Investment return from operations is defined as the investment payout according to the spending rule for the Long-Term Balanced Pool and the actual investment income for all other investments. As reflected in the Consolidated Statement of Activity, investment return as of June 30, 20X2, was as follows:

Changes in unrestricted net assets	
Operating: investment return	$ 97,875
Nonoperating: investment return reinvested	119,831
Total investment return	$217,706

....

Note X: Fair Value of Financial Instruments

The following methods and assumptions were used by the Organization in estimating the fair value of its financial instruments:

Cash and cash equivalents. The carrying amount reported in the statement of financial position approximates fair value because of the short maturity of those instruments.

Investments. The fair value of investments in marketable equity and debt securities is based on quoted market prices. Nonmarketable debt securities are valued based on estimated discounted future cash flows; nonmarketable equity securities are carried at estimated current value if it is possible to determine this; otherwise at cost.

Assets held by bond trustee. The carrying amount reported in the statement of financial position approximates fair value because of the short maturity of those instruments.

Contributions receivable. The fair value of contributions receivable reported on the statement of financial position approximates fair value because the receivable has been reflected net of a discount based on a risk-free rate.

Accrued interest receivable. The carrying amount reported in the statement of financial position approximates fair value because of the short maturity of those instruments.

Due from the [Related Organization]. The carrying amount reported in the statement of financial position approximates fair value due to the short-term nature of the receivable.

Loan payable. The carrying amount reported in the statement of financial position approximates fair value because the Organization can obtain similar loans at the same terms.

The estimated fair values of the Organization's financial instruments are as follows:

	Carrying Amount	Fair Value
Cash and cash equivalents	$ 3,269,674	$ 3,269,674
Investments	9,079,171	9,090,348
Assets held by bond trustee	2,102,455	2,102,455
Contributions receivable	10,499,892	10,499,892
Accrued interest receivable	49,309	49,309
Due from [*Related Organization*]	177,465	177,465
Loan payable	13,500,000	13,500,000

....

Note X: Fair Value of Financial Instruments [*portion of Accounting Policies note*]

Fair Value of Financial Instruments—The Ballet's financial instruments include cash, cash equivalents, guaranteed investment contracts, accounts receivable, pledges receivable, receivables from split-interest agreements, endowment investments, accounts payable and accrued expenses, an interest rate swap agreement, and bonds payable. For cash, cash equivalents, accounts receivable, and accounts payable and accrued expenses, the carrying amounts approximate fair value because of the short maturity of these items. Endowment investments, guaranteed investment contracts, pledges receivables, receivables from split-interest agreements, and the interest rate swap agreement are reflected at their estimated fair values using methodologies described above. The carrying amount of the bonds payable represents a reasonable estimate of the corresponding fair value due to the associated variable interest rate.

· ·

Note X: Investments

Most investments are carried at market value, as quoted on major stock exchanges. Investments with limited marketability have been valued in the manner described below, which includes recognition of risk factors as appropriate:

- Values assigned to fixed income securities are based on market values of commercial debt instruments.
- All other securities or real estate held for investment purposes are valued at estimated realizable values.

Realized and unrealized gains or losses on investments are determined by comparison of specific costs of acquisition (identified lot basis) to proceeds at the time of disposal, or market values at the balance sheet date, respectively, and include the effects of currency translation with respect to transactions and holdings of foreign securities.

· ·

Note X: Disclosures Related to Derivatives

The following examples are adapted from financial statements of major educational institutions, which are the primary users of derivatives in the not-for-profit world. Smaller organizations which use derivatives may not need such extensive disclosures. Specific information about derivatives is normally not shown separately in the basic financial statements, since assets are included within the investment caption, and gains/losses within the investment return caption.

Derivatives [*portion of Accounting Policies note*]

Derivative financial instruments are recorded at fair value with the resulting gain or loss recognized in the Statement of Activities.

Summary of Significant Accounting Policies [*portion of longer note*]

Derivative financial instruments held for investment purposes are carried at estimated fair values with resulting gains and losses included in investment return.

Derivative Financial Instruments [*portion of Accounting Policies note*]

The University's external investment managers are authorized to use specified derivative financial instruments, including futures and forward currency contracts, in managing the assets under their control, subject to restrictions and limitations adopted by the Board of Trustees.

Futures contracts, which are commitments to buy or sell designated financial instruments at a future date for a specified price, may be used to adjust asset allocation, neutralize options in securities, or construct a more efficient portfolio. The managers have made limited use of exchange-traded interest rate futures contracts. Margin requirements are met in cash; however the managers settle their positions on a net basis and, accordingly, the cash requirements are substantially less than the contract amounts. Forward currency contracts, which are agreements to exchange designated currencies at a future date at a specified rate, may be used to hedge currency exchange risk associated with investments in fixed-income securities denominated in foreign currencies and investments in equity securities traded in foreign markets. The managers settle these contracts on a net basis and, accordingly, the cash requirements are substantially less than the contract amounts. Changes in the market value of the futures and forward currency contracts are included in investment income and were not significant in 20X2 and 20X1.

The University makes limited use of interest rate swap agreements to manage interest rate risk associated with variable rate debt. Under interest rate swap agreements, the University and the counterparties agree to exchange the difference between fixed rate and variable rate interest amounts calculated by reference to specified notional amounts during the agreement period. Notional principal amounts are used to express the volume of these transactions, but the cash requirements and amounts subject to credit risk are substantially less. Amounts receivable or payable under swap agreements are accounted for as adjustments to interest expense on the related debt.

....

Note X: Investments [*portion of longer note*]

The University may employ derivatives and other strategies to (1) hedge against market risks, (2) arbitrage mispricing of related securities, and (3) replicate long or short positions more cost-effectively. Accordingly, derivatives in the investment portfolio may include currency forward contracts, interest rate and currency swaps, call and put options, debt and equity futures contracts, equity swaps, and other vehicles that may be appropriate in certain circumstances. Since [*University*] does not strive for higher returns through market timing or by making leveraged market bets, derivatives are not used for speculation.

[*University*]'s derivative positions directly held at June 30, 20X2 included interest rate swaps and currency forward contracts. The market value of these derivatives was $12.3 million. A gain of $2.5 million related to these transactions is included within total endowment return in the Statement of Activities.

....

Note X: Investments [*portion of longer note*]

The College's endowment investment portfolio includes derivative financial instruments that have been acquired to reduce overall portfolio risk by hedging exposure to certain assets held in the portfolio. The endowment also employs certain derivative financial instruments to replicate long or short positions more cost effectively than through purchases or sales of the underlying assets.

The College from time to time enters into foreign currency forward contracts to protect long-term investments denominated in foreign currency from currency risk. At June 30, 20X2 and 20X1, respectively, the College held forward contracts to buy foreign currencies in the amount of $34,950,000 and $17,300,560, and to sell foreign currencies in the amount of $11,500,000 and $23,980,000. The College has also recorded associated net unrealized losses of $2,300,000 and net unrealized gains of $6,107,000 on forward contracts held as of June 30, 20X2 and 20X1, respectively.

At June 30, 20X2, the College also held options and futures contracts principally as hedges against market concentration risks in certain segments of its investment portfolio. The College has recorded net unrealized gains of $450,000 and $2,466,870 as of June 30, 20X2 and 20X1, respectively, pertaining to options contracts held. The difference between the exercise price of open written options contracts and the estimated value of the related underlying securities resulted in a net short position of $650,000 and $237,000 at June 30, 20X2 and 20X1, respectively. The College is obligated to pledge to the appropriate broker, cash or securities to be held as collateral, as determined by exchange margin requirements for futures contracts held. At June 30, 20X2 and 20X1, the market value of the College's pledged collateral on futures contracts was $2,500,688 and $2,344,188, respectively. The difference between the estimated value of open futures contracts to sell and purchase securities was a net short position of $5,356,600 and a net long position of $2,322,766 as of June 30, 20X2 and 20X1, respectively.

....

Note X: Bonds and Notes Payable [*portion of longer note*]

Interest Rate Swaps

The University has entered into various interest rate swap agreements to manage the interest cost and risk associated with its variable-rate debt portfolios. During fiscal year 20X2, [*University*] entered into an additional $244 million notional principal amounts of swap agreements. Under these agreements, the University pays fixed rates, ranging from 4.3% to 6.2%, determined at inception, and receives the 3-month LIBOR on the respective notional principal amounts. The following schedule presents swap agreements in force related to this strategy at June 30, 20X2, in thousands of dollars:

	Notional Amount	Market Value	Net Interest Expense 20X2	20X1	Expiration Date
Facilities	$295,000	$(10,556)	$8,332	$344	20X3–20X4
Student loan	10,000	(112)	45	32	20X3
	$305,000	$(10,668)	$8,377	$376	

These financial instruments involve counterparty credit exposure. The policy of the University is to require collateral to the maximum extent possible under normal trading practices. The counterparties for these swap transactions are major financial institutions that meet the University's criteria for financial stability and creditworthiness.

. . . .

Note X: Debt [*portion of longer note*]

In April 20X1, the University entered into an interest rate swap agreement with a national bank to reduce its interest rate risk on a portion of its debt. The agreement extends through 20X6 and provides for the University to pay a fixed rate of 5.34% and receive a variable rate based on a notional principal amount of $34,300,000.

. . . .

Note X: Bonds Payable [*portion of longer note*]

Bonds payable at May 31, 20X2 of $3,400,000 are tax-exempt, with interest at a variable rate (3.1% during 20X2), due June 20Z5. In December of 20X1, an interest rate cap of 5% was purchased, with an expiration date of December 20X5.

. . . .

FASB Statement No. 133, *Accounting for Derivative Instruments and Hedging Activities*, requires an entity that holds a derivative financial instrument to distinguish between those designated as fair value hedges, cash flow hedges, and hedges of foreign currency exposure. FASB Statement No. 133 does not permit not-for-profit organizations to use cash flow hedge accounting.

FASB Statement No. 133 requires entities holding derivative financial instruments that have been designated and have qualified as fair value hedges to disclose the gain or loss recognized during the reporting period.

. . . .

Note X: Derivative Financial Instruments

The Organization entered into interest rate swap agreements with National Bank in order to convert the interest rates on four variable rate loans to fixed rates. Since these swap agreements do not qualify as hedging transactions, the change in value of the agreements is recognized currently as a gain. The gain in 20X2 was $135,256.

....

Note X: Interest Rate Swap

The University entered into an interest rate swap agreement to reduce economic risks associated with variability in cash outflows for interest required under provisions of variable rate bonds. Interest rate swaps are recognized as assets or liabilities at fair value. A liability of $272,500 was recognized as of June 30, 20X1. The swap was dissolved for a loss of $105,000 during 20X2. Realized gains and losses on interest rate swaps are classified as a component of operating income and presented as an adjustment to interest expense in the accompanying statement of operations. Unrealized changes in the fair value of interest rate swaps are recognized as a change in unrestricted net assets separate from excess of revenues over expenses.

....

Note X: Endowments and Split-Interest Gifts

Changes in the Organization's endowments for the year ended August 31, 20X2 are as follows:

Investment returns:	
Earned endowment income (including $2,391 reinvested in endowment, as required by donor)	$ 122,791
Change in net realized and unrealized appreciation of investments during the year	501,960
Total investment returns	624,751
Unrestricted income and gains and distributed for operations	(161,340)
Reinvested endowment returns	463,411
Other changes in endowments:	
Gifts (net of $2,054 in pledges)	67,648
Transfer to funds functioning as endowment, net	28,621
Actuarial adjustment	(5,465)
Net changes in endowments	554,215
Endowment and funds functioning as endowment, beginning of year	3,225,205
Endowment and funds functioning as endowment, end of year	$3,779,420

....

Note X: Marketable Securities and Other Investments

Marketable securities held as of December 31, 20X2 and 20X1 are as follows:

	20X2		20X1	
	Market Value	*Cost*	*Market Value*	*Cost*
Domestic equity portfolio	$1,455,185	$1,116,867	$1,092,300	$ 825,377
Foreign stock portfolio	502,760	498,026	535,332	508,406
Fixed income portfolio	814,485	789,469	718,488	715,574
TOTAL	$2,772,430	$2,404,362	$2,346,120	$2,049,357

The Organization's investment strategy incorporates certain financial instruments which involve, to varying degrees, elements of market risk and credit risk in excess of the amounts recorded in the financial statements. These instruments include securities sold but not yet purchased, loaned securities, and forward foreign currency contracts.

Securities sold but not yet purchased amounted to $78.7 and $61.2 million at December 31, 20X2 and 20X1. These securities have market risk to the extent that the Organization, in satisfying its obligation, may have to purchase securities at a higher value than recorded. The obligation to purchase securities is recorded as a liability equal to the amount of the sales proceeds, adjusted to fair value of the securities at the balance sheet date. Collateral in the form of $82.8 and $65.1 million of owned domestic securities as well as $78.5 and $60.3 million cash collateral is held by a third party at December 31, 20X2 and 20X1, respectively.

Through a securities lending program, managed by its investment custodians, the Organization loans certain marketable securities included in its investment portfolio. At December 31, 20X2 and 20X1, the market value of securities loaned was $398.9 million and $283.1 million, respectively. The custodians' loan agreements require the borrowers to maintain collateral equal to 100% to 102% of the market value of the securities loaned. This collateral in the form of cash, U.S. Treasury Bills, or guaranteed letters of credit is revalued on a daily basis.

The Organization enters into forward contracts in order to manage its foreign currency exchange risk. At December 31, 20X2 and 20X1, the Foundation had open commitments with a market value of $231.3 million and $33.3 million, respectively, which approximate contract values. Such contracts involve, to varying degrees, risk of loss arising from the possible inability of the counterparties to meet the terms of the contracts. These investments are recorded as marketable securities, included in the foreign stock portfolio.

Private equity investments held as of December 31, 20X2 and 20X1 are as follows:

	Market Value	*Cost*
20X2	$245,381	$199,572
20X1	214,867	202,421

The Organization uses a number of outside parties in the management of its marketable securities and private equity investment portfolios. Fees of $11.9 million and $8.0 million related to these services are included in the statements of operations as expenses for 20X2 and 20X1, respectively.

Real estate investments, which are located primarily in Florida and New York, as of December 31, 20X2 and 20X1, are as follows:

	Appraised Value	*Acquisition Value*
20X2	$527,977	$440,778
20X1	641,336	589,805

....

Note X: Real Estate Investments

Real estate investments consist of unimproved land, improved properties, long-term ground leases, and interests in real estate partnerships.

In accordance with Section 4942 of the Internal Revenue Code, the Foundation is required to determine the fair market value of its investments at least at the end of each five-year period. The Foundation adjusted the preponderance of its real estate investments to current appraised values as of December 31, 20X0. The values of real estate investments are determined primarily by independent appraisals and reviewed and approved by management.

Because of the inherent uncertainties of the real estate valuation, the appraised values reflected in the financial statements may differ significantly from values that would be determined by negotiations between parties in sales transactions, resulting in differences that could be material.

Gains on real estate sales are recognized at the time of sale or revaluation, or on the installment method, in accordance with generally accepted accounting principles. Gains are recorded in comparing acquisition values to the proceeds from the sales. Acquisition value represents value at date of receipt. The Foundation's share of earnings or losses of real estate partnerships is recognized using the equity method of accounting.

....

Note X: Investments

Investments are carried at market value. In accordance with the Organization's policy, significant real estate investments are stated at most recent appraised value. Significant real estate investments are appraised every five years, most recently in 20X1. The market value of additions to real estate investments between appraisal dates is considered equal to cost.

....

Note X: Endowment Investments [*portion of longer note*]

A member of the Foundation's Board of Directors is a General Partner of the limited partnership. A member of the Ballet's Board of Trustees is the Chief Executive Officer of the Foundation's investment custodian.

....

Note X: Program-Related Investments

Notes receivable consist primarily of loans made to nonprofit organizations as a means of assisting them in achieving charitable objectives such as the preservation of open space and the development of low-income housing. Interest rates on the notes receivable at December 31, 20X2, range from 7% to 10%.

In accordance with Section 4944 of the Internal Revenue Code, the Foundation is permitted to make investments that are related to its philanthropic programs. These investments are anticipated to have a less than fair market value return. In the year of the investment, the Foundation receives a credit toward its mandatory payout requirement. When the investment is recovered by the Foundation, it is required to recognize a negative distribution.

....

Note X: Security Lending Agreements

At June 30, 20X2 and 20X1, the Organization held $124,000,000 and $97,560,000, respectively, of short-term U.S. Government obligations and cash as collateral deposits for certain securities loaned temporarily to brokers. These amounts are included as assets and liabilities in the Organization's financial statements. Also, at June 30, 20X2 and 20X1, certain security loans were collateralized by lines of credit of $225,000 and $855,000, respectively. Securities on loan at June 30, 20X2 and 20X1 had estimated market values of $119,000,000 and $98,500,000, respectively.

....

Note X: Subsequent Event—Change in Market Value

Subsequent to June 30, 20X2, volatility experienced in the financial markets has resulted in a significant decline in the market value of certain investments. As of October 31, 20X2, the market value of the investment portfolio declined by approximately $11,737,000 from June 30, 20X2.

INVESTMENT PAYOUT, INCLUDING THE TOTAL RETURN CONCEPT

See also a sample disclosure in Chapter 2 of this publication regarding investment expenses. Additional discussion of this subject is at paragraphs 8 through 13 of FASB

Statement No. 124, and paragraphs 8.09-.10, 8.12-.13, and 8.16-.22 of the AICPA Audit and Accounting Guide *Not-for-Profit Organizations.* Readers should also be aware that state laws differ in this area and any given example of a disclosure may not be acceptable in some jurisdictions. Another point that is sometimes overlooked is stated in paragraph 11 of FASB No. 124, namely that if the donor of an endowment fund stipulates a purpose for the current income (interest and dividends) but is silent about the use of capital gains, there is a presumption that the gains carry the same restriction as the income—again, assuming state law does not impose a different requirement.

Note X: Investments

Because Endowment investment funds include funds derived originally from permanently restricted gifts, the management of these funds is subject to [State] law. The Board has interpreted state law as requiring the preservation of the historical dollar value of these permanently restricted gifts. After maintaining this value, the Board interprets the law as allowing it to use any of the investment returns as is prudent considering the Association's long- and short-term needs, expected total return on its investments, price level trends, and general economic conditions.

In accordance with this interpretation, the Organization has adopted an investment policy that establishes the long-term objective of achieving an annualized total investment return of 5%, net of its spendable objective. The annual spendable objective, which is used to provide funds for operating and capital expenditures, and is calculated as 5% of the average market value of assets over the 12-quarter period ending on the prior December 31, is to be met through the use of interest, dividends, and, to the extent appropriate, accumulated capital gains.

The summary of Endowment investment results, net of investment management fees, for the years ended June 30, 20X2 and 20X1, is as follows:

	20X2	20X1
Annualized rate of total return on investments (interest, dividends, and market appreciation)	17.9%	21.7%
Return on investments:		
Interest and dividends	$ 1,963	$ 1,718
Expended capital gains	1,714	1,652
Total spendable objective	3,677	3,370
Retained capital gains	10,283	11,387
Total	$13,960	$14,757
Amount utilized for operating and capital expenditures as a percentage of beginning market value of investments	4.3%	4.8%

The annualized rate of total return on these investments, net of investment management fees, is computed as the annualized sum of each quarter's total investment returns, included unrealized gains, divided by the sum of the year's beginning fair market value plus the weighted average of net quarterly additions.

....

Note X: Investment Return

The investment portfolios of all funds are carried at fair value at July 31, 20X2. Interest and dividend income is presented net of investment advisory fees. Investment advisory fees and other investment management expenses paid by the Organization were approximately $1,704,000 for the year ended July 31, 20X2. All investment income is credited to unrestricted net assets unless otherwise stipulated by the donor. All capital appreciation/depreciation earned on investments related to unrestricted funds is credited to unrestricted net assets, and on temporarily restricted funds to temporarily restricted net assets, unless otherwise stipulated by the donor. If a donor has restricted the income from a fund but has not specified the status of gains, the gains are considered to carry the same restriction as the income. In accordance with the Organization's interpretation of applicable laws, capital appreciation/depreciation earned on investments related to permanently restricted funds is credited to permanently restricted net assets to maintain the purchasing power of the donor's gift. The Organization's investments do not have a significant concentration of credit risk within any industry, geographic location, or specific institution.

....

Note X: Investment Return

The Organization's Board of Directors has approved a spending rate policy whereby a predetermined amount of investment income is established to fund current operations. The spending rate is intended to represent a reasonable return (dividends, interest, and realized gains) on the market value of the Endowment investments. The spending rate was 6.9% and 6.8% in 20X2 and 20X1, respectively.

Investment income is reported as follows:

| | For the Year Ended July 31, | |
	20X2	*20X1*
Interest and dividends	$ 4,977	$ 4,913
Portion of net realized gains applied towards authorized spending rate	3,026	3,090
Total authorized spending rate included in operating revenues	8,003	8,003
Net endowment gains in excess of authorized spending rate reported separately as a change in net assets	2,820	5,322
Total	$10,823	$13,325

....

Note X: Investment Return

The following schedule summarizes investment return by net asset classification:

	Unrestricted	Temporarily Restricted	Permanently Restricted	Total
Gross investment income	$10,845,997	$ 2,155,889	$ 6,865	$ 13,008,751
Less investment expenses	(55,710)	(12,192)	(543)	(68,445)
Net investment income	10,790,287	2,143,697	6,322	12,940,306
Net realized and unrealized gains	73,679,324	18,664,683	58,874	92,402,881
Net return on investments	84,469,611	20,808,380	65,196	105,343,187
Investment return allocated for current activities	(29,309,644)	(7,531,902)		(36,841,546)
Investment return in excess of amounts allocated for current activities	$55,159,967	$13,276,478	$65,196	$ 68,501,641

. . . .

Note X: Return on Investments

Investments at May 31, 20X2 and related investment income for the year ended May 31, 20X2 for the Organization consisted of the following:

	Investment Income	Net Unrealized Gains (Losses)	Net Realized Gains	Fair Value
Equity securities	$ 272	$ 59	$ 1,292	$ 10,730
Money market funds and other short-term investments	3,446	24	81	97,205
U.S. Treasury, government agency obligations, and corporate bonds	23,183	(3,812)	246	396,096
Other investments	1,818	544	164	14,367
	$28,719	$(3,185)	$ 1,783	$518,398

. . . .

Note X: Spending Policy

The Board of Directors of the Organization has approved a spending policy from the endowment to support operating and program expenses, major maintenance, and art acquisitions. The amount appropriated for operations and acquisitions in fiscal 20X2 was 5.0% of the total market value of the endowment averaged over the previous 12 quarters.

. . . .

Note X: Total-Return Method

The Organization makes distributions from the Endowment Fund to operations using the total-return method. Under the total-return method, Fund distributions consist of net investment income and may, under certain conditions, include a portion of the cumulative realized gains. The Board of Trustees establishes a spending rate as a percentage of the market value of endowed funds at the beginning of each fiscal year. Distributions are made in an amount equal to the product of the market value of endowed funds at the beginning of the year and the spending rate. To the extent that the distributions exceed net investment income, they are made from realized gains.

A spending rate of 5.64% for fiscal year 20X2 resulted in total distributions related to endowment funds of $14.9 million for the year ended June 30, 20X2, of which approximately $2.7 million represents transfers of realized gains from the endowment distribution reserve.

....

Note X: Endowment Payout

The Organization's policy governing the amounts paid annually from the endowment pools to support current operations is designed to protect the value of the endowment against the expected impact of inflation and to provide real growth of the endowment, while also funding a relatively constant portion of the Organization's current operating expenditures. The payout rate, set annually by the Board, is based on an estimate of total investment returns and the expected impact of inflation on the endowment assets. The sources of the payout are earned income on the endowment assets (interest, dividends, rents, and royalties), previously reinvested income, and a portion of realized capital gains.

The Board approved a payout rate of 5.25% for fiscal years 20X2 and 20X1. To meet the Board-authorized payout rate, previously reinvested income and realized gains were withdrawn, net of reinvestment, in the amount of $2,455,000 in 20X2 and $1,988,000 in 20X1.

....

Note X: Spending Rate Return

The Organization's Board of Directors has adopted a spending rate policy whereby a predetermined amount of investment income is provided to fund current operations. The spending rate return reflected in unrestricted net assets was $5,071,000 and $4,825,000 in fiscal years 20X2 and 20X1, respectively, calculated as 5.5% of the three-year rolling average market value of investments after investment management costs. In 20X2 and 20X1, net investment income included interest and dividend income, and realized and unrealized gains of $3,261,000, $9,288,000 and $1,607,000; and $3,723,000,

$5,263,000 and $4,253,000, respectively, and is net of investment expenses of $501,000 and $452,000, respectively. Unrestricted investment income also includes interest income earned on operating funds of $135,000 and $183,000 in 20X2 and 20X1, respectively.

....

Note X̄: Spending Rate

The Organization's annual draw from its unrestricted endowment funds (excluding life income instruments) is calculated as a percentage of a rolling average of the prior eight quarterly market balances and current year contributions. Effective June 1, 20X1, the Organization changed the percentage used in the endowment draw calculation from 5% to 6%. The Board approved this change through December 31, 20X2, with the option of extending it based upon the Organization's achievement of certain fund raising goals.

Subsequent Event:

In July 20X2, the [*XXX*] General Assembly of the [*State*] passed Substitute House Bill No. [*XXX*], which became law effective October 1, 20X2. Under the provisions of this Bill as interpreted by legal counsel, the Organization is permitted to expend the gains, both realized and unrealized, on its restricted endowment funds unless specifically restricted by the donor. Expenditure of such gains would include those accumulated prior to October 1, 20X2. Management is in the process of analyzing the impact and determining the effect of this new law.

[*The preceding paragraph could be presented as a separate note, possibly entitled "Change in State Law Regarding Endowment Funds."*]

....

Note X: Beneficial Interest in Assets Held by Others

In 20W5, the Organization transferred $1,000,000 from its investment portfolio to the XYZ Community Foundation to establish an endowment fund. Under the terms of the agreement, in the first quarter of each year, the Organization receives a distribution equal to the investment return generated by the transferred assets in the prior year. The Organization can withdraw all or a portion of the original amount transferred, any appreciation on those transferred assets, or both, provided that a majority of the governing boards of the Organization and the Foundation approve the withdrawal. At the time of the transfer, the Organization granted variance power to the Foundation. That power gives the Foundation the right to distribute the investment income to another not-for-profit organization of its choice if the Organization ceases to exist or if the governing board of the Foundation votes that support of the Organization is no longer necessary or is inconsistent with the needs of the community. At June 30, 20X2, the endowment fund has a value of $1,228,620, which is reported in the statement of financial position as beneficial interest in assets held by others.

CONCENTRATION OF RISK

Note X: Investments

Published market quotations do not necessarily represent realizable values, particularly where sizable holdings of a company's stock exist, as in the case of the Foundation's holding of [*Company*] common stock, which has a fair value of $[*XXX*] at the balance sheet date.

• •

Note X: Concentrations of Credit Risk

Financial instruments which potentially subject the Organization to concentrations of credit risk consist of money market accounts and investment securities.

The Organization places its temporary cash and money market accounts with creditworthy, high-quality financial institutions. A significant portion of the funds is not insured by the FDIC or related entity.

The Organization has significant investments in stocks, bonds, and mutual funds and is therefore subject to concentrations of credit risk. Investments are made by investment managers engaged by the Organization and the investments are monitored for the Organization by an investment advisor. Although the market value of investments is subject to fluctuations on a year-to-year basis, management believes the investment policy is prudent for the long-term welfare of the Organization and its beneficiaries.

• •

Note X: Concentrations of Credit Risk

Financial instruments which potentially subject the Organization to concentrations of credit risk, as defined by FASB Statement of Financial Accounting Standards No. 105, consist principally of cash. The Organization maintains its cash in various bank deposit accounts which, at times, may exceed federally insured limits. The Organization has not experienced any losses in such accounts.

• •

Note X: Concentrations of Credit Risk

Certain financial instruments potentially subject the Organization to concentrations of credit risk. These financial instruments consist primarily of cash and cash equivalents and receivables. The Organization places its cash and cash equivalents with high credit quality financial institutions. Concentrations of credit risk with respect to receivables are generally diversified due to the large number of entities and individuals composing the Organization's program and donor base. The Organization performs ongoing credit evaluations and writes off uncollectible amounts as they become known.

．．．．．．．．．．．．．．．．．．．．．．

Note X: Credit Risk

At December 31, 20X2, the Organization had deposits in a single financial institution totaling approximately $632,000 in excess of federal depository insurance limits.

．．．．．．．．．．．．．．．．．．．．．．

Note X: Concentration of Revenue Sources

Approximately 24% of the Organization's total support and revenues is provided by one contributor.

CONTRIBUTIONS RECEIVABLE

Many organizations use the term "pledges" to describe this balance sheet item. In FASB Statement No. 116, *Accounting for Contributions Received and Contributions Made,* FASB refers to them as "promises to give." Use of the word pledge in the sample notes refers to the gift itself, not the related financial statement amounts. See also the comment about "grants" versus "contributions" in the "Liabilities" section of this chapter.

See also paragraphs 5.78 and 5.81 of the AICPA Audit and Accounting Guide *Not-for-Profit Organizations* (the Guide), and paragraph 16 of Accounting Principles Board (APB) Opinion No. 21, *Interest on Receivables and Payables,* for details of these disclosure requirements. (Paragraph 5.81 of the Guide is reprinted in Appendix C of this publication.)

Paragraph 5.67 of the Guide specifies that a risk-free rate should be used to discount these receivables. The rates stated in the sample notes should not be assumed to be the appropriate rate to use at any particular future time.

Note X: Contributions Receivable

At July 31, 20X2, the Organization had $25,282,000 of contributions receivable which will be received within one year and $9,983,000 of contributions receivable which will be received in one to five years. Total amounts expected are $42,650,000, which have been discounted by $7,385,000 using a rate of 5%.

The Organization has recorded an allowance for uncollectible receivables of $168,000 and $251,000 at July 31, 20X2 and 20X1, respectively.

Contributions receivable at July 31, 20X2 include an individual pledge in the amount of $6,000,000 due in the period 20X6 through 20X8. Remaining contributions receivable are individually less than 10% of total contributions receivable at that date and are not considered to represent a significant concentration of credit risk.

At July 31, 20X2, the Organization had also received conditional promises of $9,000,000 ($1,000,000 for restoration of the theater, $5,000,000 for endowment, and $3,000,000 for purposes to be mutually agreed upon) which it expects to receive during the period 20X4 to 20X8. The receipt of such contributions is conditional on the Organization completing the restoration of the theater and the receipt of certain cash contributions from other donors.

....

Note X: Conditional Contributions Receivable

The Opera Company has an existing conditional promise to receive $80,815, due in the fiscal year ending June 30, 20X3. Payment is contingent upon meeting a certain working capital requirement, reaching a minimum operating expense level, and not incurring any long-term debt with the exception of monies intended for the acquisition of capital assets.

During fiscal 20X2, the Company received a conditional promise of $200,000, due in $100,000 increments in December 20X3 and 20X4. Payment of the first $100,000 of the grant is contingent upon the Company's ability to expand from a four-opera to a five-opera season during the fiscal year ended June 30, 20X3, which will include the performance of [*Opera A*]. The second grant payment is contingent upon the Company successfully raising during 20X2-20X3 $88,000 for the production of [*Opera A*], and $86,000 for the 20X3-20X4 production of [*Opera B*], before its opening performance in November 20X3.

As the conditions for payment by the donors of these promises have not been met as of June 30, 20X2, these amounts are not included in fiscal year 20X2 revenues and are not included in contributions receivable at June 30, 20X2.

....

Note X: Contributions Receivable

Promises to give, net of discount to present value (at a rate of 7%) and allowance for doubtful accounts, are due to be collected as follows:

	August 31	
	20X2	*20X1*
Gross amounts due in:		
One year (including $200 and $556 of endowment pledges in 20X2 and 20X1, respectively)	$ 1,974	$ 1,223
One to five years	1,194	600
More than five years	1,443	1,543
	4,611	3,366
Less discount to present value	(944)	(964)
	3,667	2,402
Less allowance for doubtful accounts	(87)	(304)
Total	$ 3,580	$ 2,098

The discount will be recognized as contribution income in fiscal years 20X3 through 20Y5 as the discount is amortized using an effective yield over the duration of the pledge.

Approximately $3,250 of the gross contributions receivable at August 31, 20X2 were due from five individuals, corporations, or foundations.

In addition, the Organization has been informed of intentions to give in the form of possible future bequests, currently of indeterminable value, that have not been reflected in the accompanying financial statements because they are not unconditional promises.

. . . .

Note X: Contributions Receivable

Contributions receivable represent unconditional promises to give by donors. Current contributions receivable are expected to be collected during the next performance year and are recorded at net realizable value. Long-term contributions receivable are expected to be collected subsequent to performance year 20X3. Contributions which are expected to be collected after one year have been discounted at 4% and are reflected in the financial statements at their net present value. Contributions receivable are due as follows:

	Performance Years	
	20X2	*20X1*
Less than one year	$4,736,053	$ 802,296
One to five years (net of discounts of $633,000)	5,006,104	—
Allowance for uncollectible contributions	(112,570)	—
Total contributions receivable	$9,629,587	$ 802,296

. . . .

Note X: Contributions Receivable

In accordance with FASB Statement of Financial Accounting Standards No. 116, contributions receivable, less an appropriate reserve, are recorded at their estimated fair value. Amounts due more than one year later are recorded at the present value of the estimated future cash flows, discounted at risk-free rates applicable to the years in which the promises were received, which range from 4% to 6%. Amortization of the discount is credited to contribution income. The expiration of a donor-imposed restriction on a contribution or endowment is recognized in the period in which the restriction expires, and the related resources then are classified as unrestricted net assets.

Contributions receivable consisted of the following as of June 30, 20X2:

Unconditional promises expected to be collected in:	
Less than one year	$ 24,411
One year to five years	48,883
More than five years	14,762
Less discount to present value ($12,074) and other reserves ($10,000)	(22,074)
Total	$ 65,982

At June 30, 20X2 there were also outstanding donor intentions to pay totaling $12,130 for general operating purposes, as follows:

Amounts due in:	
Less than one year	$ 3,693
One to five years	8,388
Thereafter	49
	$12,130

These intentions to pay are not unconditional promises and therefore have not been included in the Organization's financial statements.

· ·

Note X: Contributions Receivable

As of December 31, 20X2, the expected future cash receipts of unconditional contributions receivable are:

Receivables due in less than one year	$ 9,850
Receivables due in one to five years	7,702
Receivables due in more than five years	2,197
Less estimated uncollectible amounts	(207)
	$19,542

The Organization has reported these unconditional pledges as contributions in the accompanying combined statement of activities. The present value of the unconditional contributions receivable as of December 31, 20X2 is approximately $17,402 (discount of $2,140) using a discount rate of 5%.

....

Note X: Conditional Promises to Give

A trustee has agreed to match contributions to the Organization's endowment funds on a one-for-two basis until the total reaches $10,000,000. In addition, a contributor has pledged to contribute $500,000, conditional upon proper matching with a grant from the National Endowment for the Arts.

....

Note X: Receivables From Split-Interest Agreements

Receivables from split-interest agreements represent the estimated net present value of the Ballet's irrevocable remainder interests in a pooled income fund and various trusts held by third-party trustees. The net present value of these receivables was determined using investment returns consistent with the composition of the asset portfolios of the trusts and the pooled income fund, single or joint life expectancy from the 1983 Group Mortality Table, and discount rates determined in the years in which the agreements were first established or made known to the Ballet. The estimation of the net present value of these receivables is subjective and requires significant judgment. Due to uncertainties inherent in the estimation process, it is possible that future events in either the near or long term could materially affect the amounts reported in the consolidated statement of financial position.

OTHER RECEIVABLES

Note X: Receivables [*portion of Accounting Policies note*]

The Organization extends credit to customers of its Publications Division to encourage them to purchase books and to constituent organizations to encourage them to purchase quality assessment services from the Organization. In addition, the Organization makes loans to constituent organizations at interest rates below prevailing bank rates. These loans are unsecured and require monthly payments of principal and interest. Accrued interest on the loan balances is included in loans receivable.

Receivables are reflected on the balance sheet net of allowances for doubtful collections. The allowance for doubtful trade receivables is determined based upon an annual review of account balances, including the age of the balance and the historical experience with the customer. The allowance for loan losses is determined based upon a review of the currentness of the required loan payments and historical collection experience.

Uncollectible trade and loans receivable are charged to the respective allowance. The allowances are adjusted at year end based upon the reviews discussed above. An expense or loss is recorded at the time the allowance is adjusted.

· ·

[Additional disclosures like those under the heading "Contributions Receivable" above would also be made for the contributions portion of the receivables amount in the following note.]

Note X: Receivables

Receivables consist of:

Notes, loans, and other long-term receivables	$ 62,130,620
Student accounts and trade receivables	7,708,904
Contributions receivable	2,351,866
Accrued interest receivable	607,644
	72,799,034
Less allowance for doubtful accounts	(1,442,907)
	$ 71,356,127

Included above are $326,453 of past due notes and loans receivable.

· ·

Note X: Student Accounts Receivable

Student accounts receivable are reported net of any anticipated losses due to uncollectible accounts. The College considers an account to be past due when a student leaves mid-semester with an unpaid account balance or when a student still has an account balance after the final payment due date of the semester. Past due accounts are subject to past due letter collection efforts and are subsequently placed with third-party collection agencies. If an account balance still exists at the conclusion of the 9-to-12-month collection period, the account is written off. The collectibility of individual accounts is evaluated closely at the close of each fiscal year and the allowance for uncollectible accounts is adjusted to a level which, in management's judgment, is adequate to absorb potential losses inherent in the receivable portfolio. Historical write-off history as a percentage of outstanding receivable balances is used to help establish an appropriate allowance for uncollectible accounts. The College does not assess finance charges against student receivables that are past due.

· ·

Note X: Student Loans Receivable

Student loans receivable are reported net of any anticipated losses due to uncollectible loans. The College considers a loan to be in default when it has been past due for a period of nine months. Past due loans are subject to internal collection efforts for a period of one year and are subsequently placed with third-party collection agencies for another year. If a loan is still delinquent after the two-year collection period, the loan is assigned to the Department of Education in the case of Federal Perkins Loans or written off in the case of institutional loans. The allowance for uncollectible loans is calculated as the average of the outstanding loan balance multiplied by the cohort default rate and one half of loans in default in the case of Federal Perkins Loans and one half of loans in default in the case of institutional loans. The Federal Perkins Loan program has provisions for deferment, forbearance, and cancellation of individual loans. The deferment and forbearance provisions of the Federal Perkins Loan program are generally applied to institutional loans as well. Interest continues to accrue while the loan is placed with a collection agency. At June 30, 20X2 and 20X1, student loans receivable past due 90 days or more and continuing to accrue interest total $308,196 and $539,784, respectively. At June 30, 20X2 and 20X1, student loans receivable once accruing interest but no longer accruing interest (non-accrual) total $40,635 and $87,794, respectively.

....

Note X: Student Loans Receivable

Student loans receivable are carried at cost, less an allowance for doubtful accounts. Determination of the fair value of student loan receivables, which include donor-restricted and federally sponsored student loans with mandated interest rates and repayment terms subject to significant restrictions as to their transfer and disposition, could not be made without incurring excessive costs.

....

Note X: Note Receivable From Employee

During November 20X1, the Organization became aware that an employee had misappropriated a material amount of Organization funds during fiscal 20X1. Such misappropriation principally related to the diversion of Organization funds into the employee's personal account, and through the forgery of checks. The Board of Governors obtained a promissory note and mortgage on the individual's residence, and in December 20X2, the Organization received $49,908 from the employee in consideration for the release of the note and mortgage. The financial statements at September 30, 20X2 reflect the note receivable and adjustments to members' individual accounts receivable balances, restaurant revenues, and membership income. However, additional items, relating to cash reimbursements, payroll checks, and personal checks aggregating approximately $4,900, for which no recovery was made are included in expenses.

Management believes its investigation into this matter has resulted in a reasonable quantification of diverted funds. However, there can be no assurances that all losses to the Organization have been identified.

INVENTORY AND PREPAID EXPENSES

Similar wording would be used for most types of inventory, including those of college bookstores, museum gift shops, and so on. While not-for-profit organizations may use the last in, first out (LIFO) inventory method if they wish, in most cases there would be little incentive to do so since taxes are not normally a major concern, and the bookkeeping involved is time-consuming.

Note X: Inventories

Generally, supplies inventories purchased for use in program and supporting services are carried at the lower of first in, first out cost or market.

Whole blood, its components, plasma derivatives, and tissue are valued at the lower of average cost or market.

....

Note X: Investments in Productions

Investments in sets and costumes for future productions are recorded at the lower of cost or estimated net realizable value. Income is recognized once cost is recovered.

....

Note X: Direct Response Advertising

Direct response advertising consists primarily of telemarketing, production, and mailing costs for subscription sales for the upcoming opera season. At September 30, 20X2, and 20X1, $251,379 and $492,461, respectively, of advertising which is considered to have future benefit were recorded as a prepaid asset. Noncapitalized advertising costs are charged to expense as incurred. Advertising expense was $3,886,029 and $3,693,600 in 20X2 and 20X1, respectively.

COLLECTIONS

See also the examples from Chapter 7 of the AICPA Audit and Accounting Guide *Not-for-Profit Organizations* in Appendix C of this publication. The majority of museums do not capitalize their collections, but a significant minority of museums do. Some institutions capitalize some, but not all, collection items. Note that certain disclosures are required, even if collections are not capitalized.

Note X: Art Collection

In accordance with the practice commonly followed by art museums, art objects purchased, donated, and bequeathed are included in permanently restricted net assets at a value of $1. Contributions for the purchase of art objects are reported as nonoperating support and the cost of all art objects purchased and the proceeds from deaccessions of art are reported as nonoperating items in the statement of activities.

The Museum's policy is to maintain and continue to acquire significant works of Twentieth Century and contemporary art. From time to time, objects may be deaccessioned, subject to the terms of any applicable gift documents or bequests. Deaccessions may also result when a comprehensive evaluative process deems objects are no longer useful or relevant to the purposes and activities of the Museum. Deaccessions occur solely for the advancement of the Museum's mission and all proceeds are used to strengthen and improve other areas of the collection.

The market value of the collection objects approximated $200 million at September 30, 20X2.

....

Note X: Art Collection

The Museum's art collection is made up of contemporary art objects that are held for exhibition and various other program activities. Each of the items is cataloged, preserved, and cared for, and activities verifying their existence and assessing their condition are performed continuously. The collections are subject to a policy that requires proceeds from their sales to be used to acquire other items for collections.

Purchased items are capitalized at cost; donated items at the fair value (usually determined by a professional appraisal) at the date of receipt from the donor. Items which by donor stipulation may never be deaccessioned are classified in the permanently restricted class of net assets.

....

Note X: Collections

All contributions of works of art, historical treasures, and similar assets, whether held as part of a collection or for other purposes, have been recognized at their estimated fair value at the date of receipt based upon appraisals or similar valuations. All such items, whether contributed or purchased, have been capitalized.

....

Note X: Art Collection

The art collection, which was acquired through purchases and contributions since the Museum's inception, is not recognized as an asset on the statement of financial position. Purchased collection items are recorded as decreases in unrestricted net assets in the year in which the items are acquired, or in temporarily or permanently restricted net assets if the assets used to purchase the items are restricted by donors; contributed collection items are excluded from the financial statements. Proceeds from deaccessions or insurance recoveries are reflected as increases in the appropriate net asset classes. The Museum received donated art objects valued at approximately $775,000 during the year ended June 30, 20X2.

....

Note X: Art Collection

Works of art in the Museum's collection are not recognized as assets on the statement of financial position. Purchases of artworks are recorded as decreases in unrestricted net assets in the year in which the items are acquired, or as temporarily restricted net assets if a donor makes a contribution intended to fund the subsequent purchase of artwork. Contributions of works of art are not reflected on the financial statements.

Sculpture Garden

In 20X2, the Museum entered into a 25-year agreement with the [*City*] Park and Recreation Board to jointly operate the Sculpture Garden on acreage adjacent to the Museum. The acreage and improvements thereon are property of the Park Board, which is responsible for the maintenance and security of the Garden. Sculpture placed in the Garden is the property of or is loaned to the Museum, which is financially responsible for placing, maintaining, and insuring it. Expenses related to maintaining the artwork as well as artistic programs and events occurring in the Garden are included in operations.

....

Note X: Collection

The Museum's collection comprises approximately 27,500 objects related to religious and cultural history, including paintings, sculpture, works on paper, photographs, ethnographic material, archaeological artifacts, numismatics, ceremonial objects, and broadcast media materials. The collection is held for exhibition, education, and research and is administered and stored in accordance with a formal collection management policy approved by the American Association of Museums. The Museum maintains a policy that requires the proceeds from the sale of collection objects (deaccessions) be used to acquire other items for the collection. During the year, the Museum sold several pieces from its fine arts collection, the proceeds aggregating $55,683.

....

Note X: Library, Art, and Garden Collections

The collections which were acquired through purchases and contributions since the Organization's inception are not recognized as assets on the statement of financial position. The collections are held for public education or research in furtherance of public service rather than financial gain.

Purchases of collection items are recorded as decreases in unrestricted net assets in the year in which the items are purchased, or in temporarily restricted net assets if the assets used to purchase the items are restricted by donors. Contributed collection items are not reflected on the financial statements. The estimated fair value of contributed collection items amounted to $1,600,000 in fiscal year 20X2.

The Organization continually reviews its collections and may deaccession or acquire additional items. Proceeds from deaccessions are classified as unrestricted, except when donor restrictions apply. The collections are subject to a policy that requires proceeds from deaccessioning to be used to acquire other items for collections.

FIXED ASSETS

While not-for-profit organizations may use accelerated depreciation if they wish, very few do, since taxes are not usually a concern.

Note X: Plant Facilities

Plant facilities (including land), dedicated to educational purposes, are stated at cost, or fair value at date of donation. Interest for construction financing is capitalized as a cost of construction. Art objects and collections are not capitalized, as the University uses the proceeds from any sales of such items to acquire other art or collection pieces.

Depreciation is computed using the straight-line method over the estimated useful lives of the plant assets. The estimated useful lives are:

Buildings	40 years
Building improvements	15 years
Equipment and books	6 years

Depreciation related to auxiliary activities is recorded as an auxiliary expense.

....

Note X: Capital Assets

Capital assets are summarized by major classification as follows:

	20X2	20X1
Land	$ 115	$ 115
Warehouses	1,618	1,546
Leasehold improvements	9,635	8,823
Furniture and fixtures, including data processing equipment	4,612	4,372
Theatrical equipment	9,412	7,971
Equipment held under capital lease	494	—
Construction-in-progress	636	1,691
	26,522	24,518
Less: Accumulated depreciation and amortization	(8,234)	(6,428)
	$18,288	$ 18,090

The cost of certain Government-owned equipment and facilities, which are utilized by the Organization in connection with its theatrical performances under agreements with the Government, is not reflected in the balance sheet.

[*Although not required, accumulated depreciation and amortization may be presented for each component of capital assets. This would result in a multi-columnar presentation for each year.*]

....

When grants include amounts for the acquisition of fixed assets, the funder may retain legal title to the assets, or the right to determine their disposition at the end of the grant period. In such cases, if it is probable that the recipient will be permitted to keep and use the assets over their entire useful lives, the recipient should capitalize and depreciate the assets in the normal manner for generally accepted accounting principles (GAAP) financial statements (even though the acquisition of the assets may be reported as an expenditure of the entire amount in reports to the funder). This treatment is discussed further in paragraph 9.04 of the AICPA Audit and Accounting Guide *Not-for-Profit Organizations*. Disclosure of such arrangements should be made.

Note X: Property and Equipment

Property and equipment acquired with [*Funder*] money are considered to be owned by the Organization while used for general operations. However, [*Funder*] has the right to determine the use of these assets or the use of any proceeds resulting from the sale of these assets.

The cost of property and equipment purchased in excess of $500 is capitalized. Depreciation and amortization are provided in amounts sufficient to amortize the cost of the property and equipment over the estimated useful lives of the assets (ranging from 3 to 25 years) on a straight-line basis.

[*The above would normally be part of a longer note, detailing the components of property and equipment, including cost and useful lives by category.*]

....

Note X: Current Plant Construction

At June 30, 20X2, the University had under construction buildings that will cost approximately $27.5 million. The estimated cost to complete this construction is $11.1 million. Costs incurred through June 30, 20X2 of $16.4 million are included in land, buildings, and equipment. These buildings are being funded by loans, gifts (received or promised), and grants.

....

Note X: Renovation and Expansion Project

After completion of a feasibility study that was begun in 20X1, the Project commenced with the acquisition of two adjacent parcels of property in February 20X2. Plans called for the demolition of certain structures on the acquired property, the renovation of the auditorium, public accommodations, and support areas in [*Concert Hall*], and the expansion of the facility through new construction, transforming the facility from a concert hall into a year-round music center (the "Symphony Center"). This goal will be accomplished through improvements to acoustics, performance spaces, audience entities, and support facilities, and the establishment of a new music education center.

Real estate acquisition, construction, and renovation, currently projected to cost approximately $114 million, began in earnest during May of 20X2. It is expected to be substantially completed by the fall of 20X3 and is to be financed primarily through the issuance of debt. As of June 30, 20X2 and 20X1, capitalized costs consist of the following:

	20X2	*20X1*
Real estate:		
Land	$25,025	$25,025
Building	515	515
Feasibility study	559	559
Construction and renovation (including design and other related costs)	43,528	13,715
Capitalized interest (net)	2,711	1,150
	72,338	40,964
Less: accumulated depreciation	(65)	—
Total	$72,273	$40,964

....

Note X: Land and Buildings

The value of land and certain buildings occupied or operated by the Museum is not included in the accompanying balance sheet. Title to such land and buildings is held by the Commissioners of [*Park*]. The Museum records contribution revenue and occupancy expense each year in an amount estimated to be the fair value of the use of this property.

The cost of the Student Education Center and building improvements represent major capital expenditures made by the Museum which extend programs and improve exhibition facilities for the collection and are capitalized at cost and are being amortized over their useful lives of from 10 to 30 years.

....

Note X: Land and Buildings

Included in fixed assets are land and buildings owned by the [*City*]. These City-owned properties, approximately $20,200,000 market value at date of donation ($7,500,000, net of accumulated depreciation at December 31, 20X2), have been recorded in the financial statements because, although title is held by the [*City*], the full economic value of their use is now and will continue to be in perpetuity, held by the [*Botanical Garden*]. The land and buildings which are of single-purpose design, and are dedicated solely to the Garden's use, have been provided to the Garden in accordance with the original 18XX Act of Incorporation of the [*State*], as amended, which specifies that the [*City*] will provide grounds and buildings for the Garden and that such grounds and buildings shall be under the management and control of the Garden. Further, since the original buildings were constructed, the Garden has financed various additions and improvements to the buildings which have been recorded at cost. Because the Garden does not have the power to dispose of these properties, their related equity is included in the restricted classes of net assets (permanently for nondepreciable assets—land; temporarily for depreciable assets—buildings and improvements).

....

Note X: Conservation Land

Land donated with restrictive covenants in the deed which prohibit the [*Conservation Organization*] from ever developing or disposing of the land, is recorded at fair value at the date of donation in the permanently restricted class of net assets.

....

Note X: Scenery and Costumes

The Opera's policy is to expense all the costs of scenery and costumes for a production in the fiscal year that the production is first performed. These items have been included in the accompanying statements of financial position in the amount of $1 in order to recognize the ongoing benefit of such items, which are insured in the amount of $3,000,000. Scenery and costume expenses recognized as expense totaled $790,173 and $604,031 in fiscal years 20X2 and 20X1, respectively.

. . . .

See FASB Statement No. 93, *Recognition of Depreciation by Not-for-Profit Organizations*, paragraphs 35 and 36, for a discussion of when it may be appropriate to not depreciate certain assets.

Note X: Musical Instruments

The cost (or donated value) of musical instruments is capitalized and depreciated over their estimated useful lives, except for antique musical instruments valued at $1,501,000 in 20X2 and 20X1 which are not being depreciated because their service potential is considered to last indefinitely.

LIABILITIES

In Chapter 7, see "Expenses" for tax-related items; see "Split-Interest Agreements, Including Related Assets and Liabilities" for annuity liabilities; and see "Earned Income and Deferred Revenue" for deferred revenue items.

The term "grants payable" is often used to describe amounts awarded by a funder (which may be a government, a for-profit, or a not-for-profit organization) to a not-for-profit (and, rarely, to a for-profit) recipient. This term, however, is used rather loosely in practice to refer both to contributions, as defined in FASB Statement No. 116, as well as to amounts which are not contributions, but rather payments for goods or (more often) services to be rendered by the recipient to the payor— properly referred to as exchange transactions. Because accounting by both the funder and the recipient for contributions and exchange transactions is quite different, to make it clear which kind of transaction is being described this publication uses the term "contributions payable" when that is what is intended. The term "grant" is used here to refer to the award itself, not the related financial statement amounts.

Note X: Contributions to Others

The Organization makes awards and grants for research, education, and other projects in the field of workforce development and utilization. The minimum amount for which the Organization is obligated is recorded upon the board of directors' approval. Awards and grants payable beyond one year are reported at the present value of their estimated future cash flows using a discount rate of 5%, which approximates the Organization's rate of return on U.S. government securities.

[*Although APB Opinion No. 21 requires the use of the organization's borrowing rate to discount long-term payables, many not-for-profit organizations, especially those which make grants to others, do not borrow, so their "borrowing rate" would not be known. In some cases, this rate may be approximated by using the rate of return on investments.*]

For the years ended December 31, 20X2 and 20X1, grants were awarded to charitable organizations under the following program services:

	20X2	20X1
Community vitality	$13,239,463	$10,952,186
Future work force	9,633,625	8,290,427
Involved employees	1,373,720	1,141,099
Public policy and marketplace issues	1,564,810	1,269,000
	$25,811,618	$21,652,712

Contributions payable of $6,767,000, net of unamortized discount of $875,000, as of December 31, 20X2, for which all conditions have been met, are payable in the following years:

20X3	$4,049,000
20X4–20X8	2,351,000
After 20X8	367,000
	$6,767,000

Conditional promises to give are recognized when the conditions on which they depend are substantially met. The Foundation has outstanding conditional grant commitments of $1,050,000 as of December 31, 20X2, which are dependent on the recipient organization's ability to meet the conditions established at the time of the grant approval by the Foundation's Board of Trustees.

....

Note X: Research Grant Contributions Payable

Research grant contributions payable at June 30, 20X2 consist of:

Gross contributions payable	$ 51,119,414
Less: Unamortized discount to present value	(3,556,826)
	$ 47,562,588

The gross amounts of the payables are due as follows:

Less than one year	$ 25,736,878
One to five years	25,382,536
	$ 51,119,414

At June 30, 20X2 there are outstanding intentions to pay research grants, as follows:

Less than one year	$ 2,500,000
One to five years	10,124,187
	$12,624,187

These research grant intentions to pay are not unconditional promises to pay and therefore have not been included in the Foundation's financial statements.

....

Note X: Awards and Grants to Others

Under the terms of agreements with 24 educational and medical institutions, the Organization is obligated to pay the annual stipends of 27 career professorships in [*disease*] research. The Organization also grants other research and professional education awards covering periods of up to five years.

The aggregate amount for which the Organization is obligated under its agreements as of December 31, 20X2 is approximately $98,398,000. The present value of the liability for awards and grants as of December 31, 20X2 is approximately $93,875,000. The discount of $4,523,000 will be recognized as an awards and grants expense in fiscal years 20X3 through 20X7 as the discount is amortized using an effective yield over the life of the awards and grants contract. The liability for awards and grants is payable as follows:

20X3	$ 67,802
20X4	22,333
20X5	5,610
20X6	2,503
20X7	150
	$ 98,398

In addition, subject to certain conditions, including, but not limited to, satisfactory scientific review in future years, the Organization is contingently liable for stipends of $11,558,327 under certain career professorship agreements it has with various educational and medical institutions.

....

Note X: Advances From Grantors

The majority of the advances are attributable to conditional contributions from the XYZ Charitable Trust, which has awarded the Organization grants to administer a National Residency Program, totaling $10,706,000, of which $10,591,000 has been received through December 31, 20X2. The Organization uses the funds received to provide grants to participating residence groups, based on pre-determined qualifying factors. Revenue is being recognized when the conditions are substantially met, that is, when the residence group meets the qualifications to receive a grant. The amount of the grants received by the Organization, not yet recognized as revenue, is $874,871.

....

In cases such as the following, the auditor may need to consider whether the organization has maintained an appropriate composition of assets. See paragraphs 3.25 through 3.27 of the AICPA Audit and Accounting Guide *Not-for-Profit Organizations.*

Note X: Loans From Endowment Fund

In September 20X0, the directors of the Organization authorized the borrowing of up to $10 million from the Endowment Fund for necessary capital improvements to the Opera House. This authorization was subsequently revised in May 20X1 to permit the use of borrowings in meeting current and future financial contingencies. The Organization had borrowings of $8,000,000 at June 30, 20X1 and $7,800,000 at June 30, 20X2 under this arrangement. Interest expense in 20X2 was $730,000 and in 20X1 was $648,000.

In September 20X2 the Executive Committee authorized a 30-day loan of up to $6,000,000 from the Endowment Fund. The Association borrowed $6,000,000 on September 14, 20X2 to repay its bank line of credit, as described in Note [*number*]. This borrowing is scheduled to be repaid in full on October 13, 20X2.

....

Note X: Liabilities Under Split-Interest Agreements

The balance at May 31, 20X2 consists of the following:

Charitable gift annuities	$1,602,946
Revocable trusts and life income funds	684,383
Total	$2,287,329

The University operates a charitable gift annuity program whereby donors receive a life income in exchange for assets conveyed to the University under an annuity contract. The University's liability under the annuity contracts, amounting to $1,602,946 at May 31, 20X2, is recorded at present value based on the donor's life expectancy. Payments to contract holders amounted to $226,356 during the year ended May 31, 20X2 and have been recorded as a reduction of the liability under split-interest agreements. Under the terms of the contracts, the assets, which are included in investments, are temporarily restricted. Actuarial gains and losses and amortization of the present value discount on annuity obligations are reflected in the statement of activities as changes in split-interest agreements.

In addition, the University acts as trustee for various revocable and irrevocable trusts. These trusts generally provide current income to the grantor or other designated beneficiary with benefits payable to the University and/or other beneficiaries from the corpus upon the death of the grantor. The trust activity is summarized as follows:

	Revocable Trusts and Life Income Funds	Irrevocable Trusts		
		Held for University (Included in Long-Term Investments)	Held For Other Beneficiaries	Total Irrevocable Trusts
Balance at June 1, 20X1	$ 729,136	$ 1,297,298	$ 479,386	$1,776,684
Additions	12,731	199,174	207,235	406,409
Investment income	21,320	44,075	1,740	45,815
Realized and unrealized gains (losses)	7,032	(11,188)	—	(11,188)
Beneficiary payments and expense	(85,836)	(304,327)	(688,361)	(992,688)
Balance at May 31, 20X2	$ 684,383	$ 1,225,032	—	$1,225,032

Note X: Medical Professional Liability Claims

The University is insured for medical professional liability claims through the combination of the Medical Professional Liability Catastrophe Loss Fund of [*State*], various commercial insurance companies, and a risk retention program.

The University accrues for estimated retained risks arising from both asserted and unasserted medical professional liability claims. The estimate of the liability for unasserted claims arising from unreported incidents is based on an analysis of historical claims data by an independent actuary.

The University has established a trust fund for the payment of its medical professional liability claims under its risk retention program. Annual contributions are made to the trust fund, at an actuarially determined rate, to provide funding for its retained risk. The assets of the trust fund are included in the accompanying financial statements.

························

Note X: Dormitory Financing

The College and the [*State*] Dormitory Authority executed a loan agreement for $35,000,000 under the Authority's $200,000,000 College and University Variable Rate Insured Revenue Bonds of 20W6 in connection with the construction of a dormitory to house approximately 400 students.

As a security for the loan, the College has pledged tuition revenues in the amount of $1,600,000 annually, granted a security interest in all fixtures, furnishings, and equipment of the new dormitory and executed a fee mortgage and leasehold mortgage on certain buildings and properties. The loan agreement also contains covenants which restrict the College's ability to incur additional debt.

Subsequent Event. On September 25, 20X2, the University refunded its 20W3 bonds, originally issued in the amount of $20 million. The new bonds, also issued in the nominal amount of $20 million, will mature in December 20X9 and carry a fixed interest rate of 4.75%.

....

Note X: Financing of Building Renovation

On September 26, 20X0, the City Industrial Development Agency (IDA) issued $4.1 million of Adjustable Rate Demand Civic Facility Revenue Bonds, the proceeds of which were used to finance a portion of the cost of the renovation of the Organization's headquarters as well as the retirement of the outstanding Civic Facility Revenue Bonds dated December 1, 20W1. The construction was completed in 20X1.

The proceeds were made available to the Organization under the provisions of a lease agreement pursuant to which the Organization leased the building to IDA and IDA leased the facility back to the Organization. The scheduled lease payments to be made by the Organization to IDA are intended to be sufficient to pay sinking-fund installments of principal and interest on the Bonds.

In connection with this renovation project, construction costs and a liability equivalent to the principal amount of the Bonds outstanding are reflected on the balance sheet. At December 31, 20X2, the Organization has drawn down $3,891,130. The balance of $208,870 is reflected on the balance sheet as a receivable. The Bonds bear interest at a variable rate, determined weekly, not to exceed 9.5%. The Organization has the option of converting to a fixed interest rate. The rate at December 31, 20X2 is 1.3%. The Bonds, which mature in 20Y1, are subject to mandatory redemption by IDA at a price equal to the principal amount thereof, together with accrued interest at the date of redemption, from the Sinking Fund, on the dates and in the principal amounts set forth in the schedule below. In addition, the Bonds are subject to optional redemption at the redemption prices set forth in the bond indenture.

The Organization's performance of its rental payments is secured by a mortgage lien on the Organization's building. Further, the payment of principal, interest, and redemption premium, if applicable, of the Bonds has been guaranteed by the Organization pursuant to a guaranty agreement.

Concurrent with the issuance of the Bonds, a bank issued a letter of credit in the amount of $4.1 million. The letter of credit contains various covenants, among which are the requirements to maintain minimum amounts of cash and a minimum debt service coverage ratio.

The payments of principal to IDA in satisfaction of the sinking-fund requirements are as follows:

20X3	$ 190,000
20X4	200,000
20X5	210,000
20X6	220,000
20X7	225,000
Thereafter	3,055,000
	$4,100,000

· ·

Note X: Long-Term Debt

Long-term debt consists of the following at May 31, 20X2:

Capital lease payable, used for computer software and equipment, due in monthly installments of $16,120, which includes a fixed rate of 4.96%. The lease matures in December 20X7.	$ 657,031
Economic Development Corporation Variable Rate Demand Revenue Bonds, used to refund an existing bond issue and pay off other debt. The effective rate is 1.11% at May 31, 20X2. Interest is payable monthly and principal is payable in varying annual installments, maturing May 20Y9.	14,425,000
Total	$15,082,031

Annual maturities of long-term debt are as follows:

20X3	$ 723,464
20X4	751,757
20X5	1,180,472
20X6	746,338
20X7	630,000
20X8 and thereafter	11,050,000
Total	$15,082,031

Interest expense for the year ended May 31, 20X2, on the above debt was $920,858.

The University had entered into an interest rate swap agreement in conjunction with a variable rate demand revenue bond issue that was refunded during the year. Realized losses on monthly settlement transactions totaled $14,755 and $81,435 for the years ended May 31, 20X2 and 20X1, respectively. The swap was dissolved during 20X2. At year end, no new swap agreements had been entered into.

On May 26, 20X2, as part of the 20X2 bond issue, the University issued and filed an intent to redeem the outstanding balance of the 20W6 bonds of $3,025,000. The proceeds from the 20X2 bond issue were put into trust on May 27, 20X2, and the related bond liability was called and redeemed on July 1, 20X2. In accordance with the bond documents, the related trust assets and bond liability were removed from the financial statements on the University effective May 31, 20X2.

....

Note X: Interest-Free Loan

In January 20X2, the Organization received an interest-free loan of $100,000 from a member of the Board of Trustees. The purpose of the loan was to pay operating expenses. The loan was repaid on December 31, 20X2. The contribution inherent in the interest-free loan has been recorded at fair value, based on an imputed interest rate of 6%, which is the organization's bank borrowing rate. Contribution revenue and interest expense of $6,000 has been reflected on the statement of activities.

....

FASB Statement No. 132(R), *Employers' Disclosures about Pensions and Other Postretirement Benefits,* permits a reduced level of disclosure for nonpublic entities (which includes not-for-profit organizations).

Note X: Pension

The Agency sponsors a noncontributory defined benefit retirement plan covering substantially all of its nonunion employees. The following table summarizes the benefit obligations, fair value of assets, and the funded status as of June 30, 20X2:

Benefit obligation	$(5,820,926)
Fair value of plan assets	3,537,183
Funded status	$(2,283,743)
Accrued benefit cost recognized in the balance sheet	$ 943,540
Accumulated benefit obligation	4,439,076
Employer contributions	243,272
Benefits paid	339,378
Net periodic pension cost	569,927
Weighted average assumptions	
Discount rate	7.0%
Expected return on plan assets	8.9
Rate of compensation increase	4.5

Plan Assets

The Agency's pension plan asset allocation is as follows:

Money market account	0.47%
Equity securities	59.68
Debt securities	34.84
Real estate	5.01

The investment policies are as follows:

1% of the fund will be set aside in the money market account. The remaining funds will be invested as follows:

55%	Equity
40%	Debt
5%	Real estate

The balance between equities and debt will be allowed to drift 5% either way before realignment is required.

Cash Flows

The Agency expects to contribute $225,000 to its pension plan in 20X3.

The following benefit payments, which reflect expected future service, are expected to be paid as follows:

20X3	$166,000
20X4	199,000
20X5	216,000
20X6	228,000
20X7	275,000
20X8–20Y2	1,441,000

....

Note X: Retirement Plans

The University maintains two contributory retirement plans for its eligible faculty and staff. The plans offer employees the choice of two investment company options, Teachers Insurance and Annuity Association (TIAA) and College Retirement Equities Fund (CREF), and the mutual funds offered by [*Investment Company*]. Participating employee and University contributions are immediately vested. The University contributed $16.7 million to the two plans in 20X2. The University also offers a noncontributory pension plan with a past service obligation that was funded over a 30-year period, with a final payment of $71,000 in fiscal year 20X2.

The University currently sponsors a health care plan permitting retirees to continue participation on a "pay-all basis," which requires a retiree contribution based on the average per capita cost of coverage for the entire plan group of active employees and retirees rather than the per capita cost for retirees only. Retirees are also eligible to participate in certain tuition reimbursement plans and may receive a payment for sick days accumulated at retirement. The University funds the benefits costs as they are incurred. Accumulated postretirement benefit obligation (APBO) at June 30, 20X2, was as follows:

Active employees not yet eligible	$ 984,000
Active employees eligible	451,000
Retirees	862,000
Unrealized loss	(190,000)
Total	$2,107,000

The components of the net periodic postretirement benefit cost were as follows:

Service cost (benefits attributed to employee service during the year)	$ 85,000
Interest cost on accumulated postretirement benefit obligation	169,000
Net periodic postretirement benefit cost	$254,000

....

Note X: Retirement Plans

Substantially all employees may elect to participate in retirement plans administered by the Teachers' Insurance and Annuity Association and/or the College Retirement Equities Fund. Under the provisions of these defined contribution pension plans, the University contributes 10% of an eligible employee's earnings. University contributions amounted to $838,074 for the year ended May 31, 20X2.

....

Note X: Summary of Significant Accounting Policies [*portion of longer note*]

Compensated Absences. Full-time employees, excluding faculty, earn from 10 to 20 days of vacation each year. Employees may be paid for up to one year's unused vacation at their current rate of pay upon termination of service. The College accrues costs incurred for vacation leave as obligations of unrestricted assets. At May 31, 20X2 and 20X1, the College had an accrual of approximately $434,000.

....

Note X: Self-Insurance Reserves

The University maintains a self-insurance program for general liability, professional liability, and certain employee and student insurance coverages. This program is supplemented with commercial excess insurance above the University's self-insurance retention. Reserves for losses under the University's self-insurance program, aggregating $27.4 million at June 30, 20X2, include reserves for known losses and for estimated losses incurred but not yet reported. A portion of the reserves pertaining to professional liability has been determined on a discounted present-value basis. Self-insurance reserves are necessarily based on estimates of historical loss experience, and while management believes that the reserves are adequate, the ultimate liabilities may be in excess of or less than the amounts provided. Under an agreement between the University and [*Medical Faculty Foundation*], a proportionate share of professional liability insurance costs is borne by the Foundation. At June 30, 20X2, the University had receivables from the Foundation of $8.8 million for its share of such costs.

....

Note X: Health Insurance Reserve

The Organization provides health insurance benefits to its employees through a partially self-funded plan. The plan is administered by a third party. The Organization self-funds the cost of the program up to specified stop-loss insurance limits. Coverage during the policy period limits the maximum individual and aggregate losses. Self-insurance costs are accrued based upon the aggregate of the liability for reported claims and an estimated liability for claims incurred but not reported. The reserve at December 31, 20X2 is $669,360.

....

Note X: Workers' Compensation

The Ballet's workers' compensation insurance policies include self-insured retention limits and fully insured coverage above such limits. Accruals for claims under the Ballet's self-insured retention limits are recorded on a claims-incurred basis. The estimated liability for workers' compensation claims at June 30, 20X2 of approximately $701,000 is included in accounts payable and accrued expenses in the accompanying consolidated statement of financial position. The estimation of the costs to be incurred for workers' compensation claims is subjective and requires significant judgment. Due to uncertainties inherent in the estimation process, it is possible that future events in either the near or long term could materially affect the amounts reported in the consolidated statement of financial position.

At June 30, 20X2, the Ballet has unused letters of credit totaling $1,835,000 and an unused security deposit of $500,000, as required by the Ballet's insurance carriers. The security deposit is included in prepaid expenses and deposits in the consolidated statement of financial position.

· ·

Note X: Costs of Discontinued Activities

On July 1, 20X2, the Organization discontinued services in its XXX facility. In accordance with FASB Statement No. 146, the organization has recorded related costs that are classified as management and general expenses. A reconciliation of the exit activity liability as of December 31, 2002 is as follows:

Balance, December 31, 2001	$ 0
Termination benefits	500,000
Lease termination costs	150,000
Accretion	8,500
Amortization	(132,500)
Balance, December 31, 2002	$ 526,000

[*In subsequent years, until and including the year that the liability is liquidated, there should be a note reconciling the opening and closing liability balances.*]

· ·

Note X: Funds Held for Others

Funds held for others consist of the following agency type accounts:

	Balance Dec. 31, 20X1	Investment Income	Principal Additions	Unrealized Gain/Loss	Distributions	Balance Dec. 31, 20X2
Other organizations' shares of:						
CRUTs	$ 1,952	$ 201	$ 1,004	$ 265	$172	$3,250
CRATs	1,797	98	—	(39)	112	1,744
Revocable trusts	685	47	—	(1)	36	695
Miscellaneous trusts	321	25	—	—	30	316
Endowment	576	42	—	(139)	25	454
Annuities	77	7	—	(2)	17	65
Temporary holding	7	—	306	11	282	42
Life insurance	41	—	263	15	—	319
	$ 5,456	$ 420	$ 1,573	$ 110	$674	$6,885

NET ASSETS

Note X: Net Assets

Unrestricted Net Assets. Unrestricted net assets consist of the following balances at August 31, 20X2 and 20X1:

	20X2	20X1
Designated for operations:		
University programs	$ 341,862	$ 240,644
Other gifts and income	309,106	304,726
Student loans and capital projects	71,161	75,986
	722,129	621,356
Investment in plant facilities	660,481	636,798
Endowment gains and funds functioning as endowment:		
Funds functioning as endowment	713,378	519,307
Gains on endowment and funds functioning as endowment	1,736,458	1,490,830
	2,449,836	2,010,137
[*Affiliated Organization*]	319,471	280,057
	$4,151,917	$3,548,348

Temporarily Restricted Net Assets. Temporarily restricted net assets contain donor-imposed restrictions that expire upon the passage of time or once specific actions are undertaken by the University. These net assets are then released and reclassified to unrestricted net assets, from which they are expended. Temporarily restricted net assets consist of the following balances at August 31, 20X2 and 20X1:

	20X2	20X1
Acquisition of capital assets	$193,248	$148,752
Term endowments	25,554	22,728
Funds subject to living trust agreements	36,585	31,544
Other gifts and income for instruction, research, and University support:		
Purpose-restricted	17,444	13,332
Time-restricted	33,719	42,691
	$306,550	$259,047

Permanently Restricted Net Assets. Permanently restricted net assets are subject to donor-imposed restrictions that the principal be invested in perpetuity. Permanently restricted net assets consist of the following balances at August 31, 20X2 and 20X1:

	20X2	20X1
Endowment funds	$1,161,275	$1,070,957
Funds subject to living trust agreements	135,566	117,181
Student loan funds	42,400	39,504
	$1,339,241	$1,227,642

....

Note X: Net Assets

Net assets consist of:

	December 31,	
	20X2	20X1
Unrestricted:		
Operating (undesignated):		
Operating reserves	40,692	67,416
Invested in equipment, net of accumulated depreciation	23,077	26,539
Less related mortgage indebtedness	(9,424)	(14,655)
Total undesignated	54,345	79,300
Designated:		
Endowment funds:		
ABC endowment	475,618	433,550
Other endowments	710,195	581,496
Charitable lead trusts receivable	987,878	1,101,838
Charitable lead trust reserves	124,102	—
Voluntary additional annuity reserves	99,442	93,170
Gift portion of annuities	381,115	421,549
Advise and consult funds	3,449,495	3,726,778
Total designated	6,227,845	6,358,381
Total unrestricted	6,282,190	6,437,681
Temporarily restricted:		
Trust funds:		
Charitable remainder unitrusts	620,575	576,201
Charitable remainder annuity trusts	36,691	39,358
Other purpose-restricted funds	41,825	178,991
Total temporarily restricted	699,091	794,550
Total net assets	6,981,281	7,232,231

....

Note X: Analysis of Restricted Net Assets

Restricted net assets consisted of the following purpose-restricted amounts as of September 30, 20X2:

	Temporarily Restricted	Permanently Restricted
Acquisition of art	$ 10,942,210	$ 56,170,104
Center for Advanced Study in the Visual Arts	918,220	11,579,168
Special exhibitions	7,077,392	744,000
Investment in fixed assets	85,555,854	—
Sculpture garden and other capital projects	6,586,896	—
Research	42,886	1,505,000
Conservation	32,798	5,650,000
Operations	780,577	69,902,300
Publications, including catalogues	870,440	—
	$112,807,273	$145,550,572

· ·

Note X: Net Assets Released From Restrictions

Net assets were released from donor restrictions when expenses were incurred to satisfy the restricted purposes specified by donors for the year ended September 30, 20X2 as follows:

	Operating	Nonoperating
Acquisition of art		$5,775,407
Center for Advanced Study in the Visual Arts	815,490	—
Special exhibitions	7,185,307	—
Depreciation of building and capital improvements	—	2,693,880
Capital projects	—	4,309,407
Research	55,604	—
Conservation	359,191	—
Operations	779,544	—
Publications, including catalogues	—	368,390
	$9,195,136	$13,147,084

· ·

Note X: Net Asset Transfers

During the year ended May 31, 20X2, net assets were transferred between permanently restricted and temporarily restricted classifications as a result of a donor's request.

· ·

Note X: Working Capital Reserves

During fiscal year 20X0, the board of trustees designated $100,000 of unrestricted net assets as a working capital reserve. The reserve may be used for cash flow management but must be replenished by June 30 of each year.

During fiscal year 20X1, the Organization received a National Arts Stabilization Fund (NASF) matching grant. The terms of the grant provide that it be used to create a restricted working capital reserve. The grant totals $323,261, payable in four installments over five years. As of June 30, 20X2, $142,446 had been matched and received by the Organization under this grant and is included in the working capital reserve as temporarily restricted net assets. As of July 1, 20X5, the end of the grant period, the funds become unrestricted and available for use at the discretion of the Organization's board of trustees.

Both reserves consist of money market funds at June 30, 20X2.

....

Note X: Endowment Fund

The Organization has maintained a national Endowment Fund since 1905 and has consistently promoted public gifts for the Fund with the understanding that the principal would be held inviolate and only the income used for current purposes. The Fund is under the control of a separate Board of Trustees who are required to keep and invest the Fund under their management. Because of public declarations regarding the use of gifts under wills, estates, and trusts, and as stated in the bylaws of the Organization, those gifts to the Organization's national sector are recorded as permanently restricted, to be kept and invested as such in perpetuity, unless the donor directs some other use of the funds.

The Fund includes contributions, some of which were accepted with specific donor stipulation that the principal be maintained intact, until the occurrence of a specific event, or for a specific period. These are reported as temporarily restricted net assets. The Fund includes additional contributions not so stipulated that resulted from appeals for Endowment Fund gifts to be managed as provided above. Based upon the manner in which the Organization has solicited and continues to solicit such gifts, it has been determined by independent legal counsel that such gifts be reported as permanently restricted net assets.

....

Note X: Endowment Fund

The Organization's Endowment Fund consists of gifts received from donors with the stipulation that the principal be invested and the income be used for the general purposes of the Organization. As of December 31, 20X2, due to declines in the market value of the investments in the Organization's portfolio, the fair value of the investments in the Endowment Fund is $240,000 less than the principal of the Endowment Fund.

....

Note X: Long-Term Reserve

The Organization's Board of Directors designated a portion of the Organization's accumulated unrestricted net assets as a long-term reserve contingency fund to be used in the event of a significant shortfall in revenues. The Board may annually direct that certain amounts of unrestricted net assets be designated as additions to the long-term reserve. During 20X2, the Board added $50,000 to the long-term reserve.

....

Because many clubs sell capital stock to their members, disclosure about such equity may be made. See also a sample Members' Equity section of a statement of financial position in Chapter 1 of this publication.

Some clubs repurchase a member's stock only when a new member has applied and paid for the stock, as disclosed in the following note.

Note X: Members' Equity

Members' equity is recorded at amounts specified in the bylaws for voting memberships. Upon the termination of a membership and the assumption of the membership by a new member, the withdrawing member is entitled to receive the greater of $3,500 or the book value of the membership ($4,239 and $4,188 at February 28, 20X2 and 20X1, respectively). As of February 28, 20X2 and 20X1 there were 12 and 14 members, respectively, who had requested termination of their membership upon application by a new member.

....

[*Other clubs will repurchase members' stock upon request, as disclosed in the following note.*]

Note X: Member Equity

The Club has agreed to purchase its members' shares at $2,250 per share when members terminate their membership in the Club. At September 30, 20X2 and 20X1, there were 287 and 274 shares, respectively, held by members. The obligation to redeem the shares is recorded as a liability on the balance sheet.

FASB Statement No. 150, *Accounting for Certain Financial Instruments with Characteristics of both Liabilities and Equities,* requires an entity that has mandatorily redeemable equity shares to recognize a liability for the redemption. However, the provisions of this Statement have been deferred.

CHAPTER 7: Sample Disclosures Related Primarily to the Statement of Activity and Related Statements

Note that these sample notes are not necessarily complete for any given organization's circumstances.

See also Chapter 6 for notes describing balance sheet amounts, many of which have effects on the statement of activity.

MEASURE OF OPERATIONS

According to Financial Accounting Standards Board (FASB) Statement of Financial Accounting Standards No. 117, *Financial Statements of Not-for-Profit Organizations,* paragraph 23, an organization may classify items as operating or nonoperating. Since this paragraph essentially permits each organization to define "operations" as it wishes, wide variety is found in practice among organizations that choose to present such a measure. Disclosure of the definition used is required. See also some of the sample statements of activities in Chapter 2 of this publication.

Note X: Measure of Operations

In its statement of activities, the Center includes in its definition of operations all revenues and expenses that are an integral part of its programs and supporting activities. Investment income, including net realized and unrealized gains and losses, earned in excess of the Center's aggregate authorized spending amount, and contributions to temporarily and permanently restricted net assets are recognized as nonoperating support, revenues, gains, and losses.

....

Note X: Measure of Operations

The Society includes in its definition of operations all income and expenditures relating to its orchestra and supporting activities. Investment income, including net realized and unrealized gains and losses, earned in excess of (or less than) the Society's authorized spending rate is recognized as nonoperating income.

....

Note X: Results of Operations

The Organization has defined a measure of operations that considers all revenues and expenses to be related to operations, except endowment gains, expendable gifts invested in the endowment, expendable capital gifts, changes in the equity of [*Affiliated Organization*], and certain other additions, which are included in the category called "other changes."

....

Note X: Measure of Operations

The Foundation includes in its measure of operations all revenues and expenses that are an integral part of its programs and supporting activities and excludes permanently restricted contributions, contributions for capital construction and art acquisition, realized and unrealized gains and losses on investments, and changes in net assets related to collection items not capitalized.

....

Note X: Measure of Operations

ABCD Organization includes in its measure of operations:

- All revenues and expenses that are an integral part of its programs and supporting activities,
- Net assets released from restrictions to support operating expenditures,
- An amount equal to 5% of the average value of endowment assets (restricted and unrestricted assets designated for long-term investment) at the end of the prior four fiscal quarters, and
- An amount equal to the lower of the average unrestricted bequests over the immediate past five fiscal years, or the unrestricted bequests in the current fiscal year.

ABCD excludes from its measure of operations:

- Contributions from and changes in the value of split-interest agreements,
- Investment return, net of amounts made available for operating purposes,
- Additions to permanently restricted net assets, and
- Bequests in excess of the immediate past-five-fiscal-year average.

CONTRIBUTIONS RECEIVED, INCLUDING GOVERNMENT GRANTS

See also the examples relating to contributions receivable in Chapter 6.

FASB Statement No. 116, *Accounting for Contributions Received and Contributions Made*, allows organizations a choice of how to report:

1. Purpose-restricted gifts and investment income whose purpose is accomplished in the same year as received—either as unrestricted revenue, or as temporarily restricted revenue and as net assets released from restrictions.

2. Donated fixed assets and donated cash restricted for the acquisition of fixed assets—as revenue either ratably over the useful life of the assets, or in full immediately upon placing the assets in service.

The method used must be disclosed.

These methods are illustrated below.

Note X: Contributions

The Organization reports gifts of cash and other assets as restricted support if they are pledged or received with donor stipulations that limit the use of the donation. When a donor restriction expires, that is when a stipulated time ends or purpose restriction is accomplished, temporarily restricted net assets are reclassified as unrestricted net assets and reported in the statement of activities as net assets released from restriction. All long-term contributions receivable at June 30, 20X2, represent temporarily restricted net assets and are due in one to five years.

Contributed assets are recorded at fair value when the Organization obtains possession or an unconditional promise to give. Contributed professional services are reflected in the financial statements. However, a substantial number of volunteers have donated their time to the program services and fund-raising campaigns of the Organization, which is not reflected in the financial statements inasmuch as applicable recognition criteria are not met.

Gifts of long-lived assets without explicit donor restrictions are reported as temporarily restricted support. The value of the long-lived asset is released from restriction ratably over the useful life of the asset.

Donor-restricted contributions whose restrictions are met in the same reporting period are reported as unrestricted contributions.

....

Note X: Accounting for Contributions

All contributions are considered to be available for unrestricted use unless specifically restricted by the donor. Amounts received that are designated for future periods or are restricted by the donor for specific purposes are reported as temporarily restricted or permanently restricted support that increases those net asset classes. Unconditional promises to give, which do not state a due date, are presumed to be time-restricted by the donor until received and are reported as temporarily restricted net assets.

A donor restriction expires when a stipulated time restriction ends, when an unconditional promise with an implied time restriction is collected, or when a purpose restriction is accomplished. Upon expiration, temporarily restricted net assets are reclassified to unrestricted net assets and are reported in the statement of activities as net assets released from restrictions. Restricted contributions received in the same year in which the restrictions are met are recorded as an increase to restricted support at the time of receipt and as net assets released from restrictions. Permanently restricted net assets include the principal amount of contributions accepted with the stipulation from the donor that the principal be maintained in perpetuity and only the income from investment thereof be expended for either general purposes or a purpose specified by the donor.

························

Note X: Revenue Recognition and Deferred Revenue

Contributions received are considered to be available for use unless specifically restricted by the donor. Conditional contributions are recognized as revenue when the conditions on which they depend have been substantially met. Contributions are recorded at fair value which is net of estimated uncollectible amounts.

The Organization records contributions as temporarily restricted if they are received with donor stipulations that limit their use either through purpose or time restrictions. When donor restrictions expire, that is, when a time restriction ends or a purpose restriction is fulfilled, temporarily restricted net assets are reclassified to unrestricted net assets and reported in the statement of activities as net assets released from restrictions. It is the Organization's policy to record temporarily restricted contributions, as well as donor-restricted income earned on permanently restricted net assets, received and expended in the same accounting period, in the unrestricted net asset class.

Contributions that the donor requires to be used to acquire long-lived assets (for example, land, buildings, leasehold improvements, furniture, fixtures, and equipment) are reported as temporarily restricted until the long-lived assets have been acquired and placed in service, at which time the Organization reflects the expiration of the donor-imposed restriction as a reclassification included in net assets released from restrictions.

························

Note X: Revenues, Expenses, Gains, and Losses

Revenues are reported as increases in unrestricted net assets unless use of the related assets is limited by donor-imposed restrictions. Expenses are reported as decreases in unrestricted net assets. Gains and losses on investments and other assets or liabilities are reported as increases or decreases in unrestricted net assets unless their use is restricted by explicit donor stipulation or law. Expiration of temporary restrictions on net assets (that is, the donor-stipulated purpose has been fulfilled and/or the stipulated time period has elapsed) are reported as reclassifications between applicable classes of net assets.

Contributions, including unconditional promises to give, are recognized in the period received. Conditional promises are not recognized until they become unconditional, that is when the conditions on which they depend are substantially met. Contributions of assets other than cash are recorded at estimated fair value. Contributions to be received after one year are discounted at an appropriate discount rate commensurate with the risk involved. Amortization of discount is recorded as additional contribution revenue in accordance with donor-imposed restrictions, if any, on the contributions. An allowance for uncollectible contributions receivable is provided based upon management's judgment including such factors as prior collection history, type of contribution, and nature of fundraising activity.

Expendable contributions received with donor-imposed restrictions are reported as revenues of the temporarily restricted net asset class. Contributions of land, buildings, and equipment without donor-imposed restrictions concerning the use of such long-lived assets are reported as revenues of the unrestricted net asset class.

....

Note X: Revenues

Membership dues, which are essentially contributions, are recognized as revenue when such income is received. General support, including endowment gifts and pledges as well as any other unconditional promises to give, is recognized as revenue in the period promised, net of estimated uncollectible amounts, which were approximately $425,000 during the year ended June 30, 20X2. Amounts expected to be collected within one year are recorded at their net realizable value, and amounts expected to be collected beyond one year are recorded at the present value of estimated future cash flows. The discount on those amounts is computed using a risk-free interest rate applicable to the year in which the promise is received. Amortization of the discount is included in general support. An allowance for uncollectible amounts is determined using the age of the receivable, creditworthiness of parties, and historical collection experience.

The Organization reports general support, including cash, as either temporarily or permanently restricted if such support is received with donor stipulations that limit the use of the donated assets. When a donor restriction expires, that is, when a stipulated time restriction ends or purpose restriction is accomplished, temporarily restricted net assets are reclassified to unrestricted net assets and reported in the statement of activities as net assets released from restrictions. However, if a donor restriction expires in the same reporting period that the contribution was made, such contribution is reported as unrestricted support in the statement of activities.

....

Note X: Contributions

All contributions are considered to be available for unrestricted use except endowment or other funds specifically restricted by the donor. Contributions are received principally by the Organization's Chapters and are shared with National Headquarters in accordance with the Organization's policy. Approximately 50% of gross contributions received during the years ended June 30, 20X2 and 20X1 were allocated to National Headquarters to support national research programs and other program services and related supporting services.

Bequests

The Organization records bequest income at the time it has an established right to such bequest and the proceeds are measurable. Bequests are received principally by the Organization's National Headquarters and are shared with the Organization's Chapters.

....

Note X: Bequests

Under guidelines established by its Board of Directors, the Organization earmarks an amount equal to 90% of total unrestricted bequests received for long-term investment, subject to its annual operating requirements. Accordingly, in the year ended September 30, 20X2, $2,293,747 from the change in unrestricted net assets from operations and $3,068,198 from nonoperating income was designated for long-term investment. In the year ended September 30, 20X1, $1,450,093 from the change in unrestricted net assets from operations and $1,730,031 from nonoperating income was designated for long-term investment.

....

Note X: Campaign

An annual fund-raising campaign is conducted each fall to obtain donations and pledges to fund the subsequent year's operations. Accordingly, a receivable is recorded at year-end for outstanding campaign pledges with an allowance for amounts estimated to be uncollectible. Substantially all of the pledges receivable at June 30, 20X2 are from corporations and individuals. The Federation maintains reserves for potential uncollectible pledges which, in the aggregate, have not exceeded management's expectations. After two years, uncollected campaign pledges are written off.

Donor-designated pledges are accounted for as a liability until disbursed to the designated agency. These amounts are not recorded as revenue by the Federation, but are reported as part of Campaign Results, from which the amounts are then deducted to arrive at Campaign Revenue.

....

Note X: Outstanding Legacies

The Organization is the beneficiary under various wills and trust agreements, the total realizable amounts of which are not presently determinable. The Organization's share of such bequests is recorded when the probate courts declare the testamentary instrument valid and the proceeds are measurable.

....

Note X: Contributions

Contributions, bequests, and specific-purpose contributions included in nonoperating revenues are as follows:

	For the Year Ended June 30,	
	20X2	20X1
Government agencies:		
National Endowment for the Arts	$ 1,079	$ 1,225
[*State*] Council on the Arts	448	400
[*City*] Department of Cultural Affairs	206	204
	1,733	1,829
Foundations and corporate support:		
Foundations (excluding new production funding)	1,613	1,661
[*Performing Arts Center*] Corporate Drive	1,572	1,677
Corporations (excluding new production funding)	1,220	1,151
	4,405	4,489
Individuals and other organizations:		
The [*XXX*] Opera Guild	7,305	9,921
Patrons	10,621	8,172
Subscribers	190	407
Major gifts	5,564	5,142
[*XXX*] Opera Fund	1,673	949
Raffle	521	873
New production funding	3,550	6,150
Galas and benefits	4,124	2,838
Special project funding	1,173	1,877
Bequests	2,601	546
Other	856	390
	38,178	37,265
	$44,316	$ 43,583

....

Note X: Federated Fund-Raising Agreements

The Organization's Divisions have agreements with various United Way agencies across the United States to participate in solicitations for contributions from employees of businesses and industrial communities.

The amount the Organization recognized as support from the United Way campaigns of approximately $36,664,000 for the fiscal year ended June 30, 20X2 is based primarily upon formulas contained in the agreements. These amounts are net of United Way fund-raising expenses. The Divisions received approximately $4,893,000 from other fund-raising organizations for the fiscal year ended June 30, 20X2.

Note X: Federated Services

Support from the public received through allocations from federated services was:

	20X2	20X1
United Way of [*City*]	$2,032,539	$2,062,542
United Way of [*Region*]	258,273	259,078
United Way of [*County*]	135,820	166,333
Other	271,132	296,913
	$2,697,764	$2,784,866

The $2,697,764 shown above was pledged to the Organization before September 30, 20X2 and has been recorded as "public support" in the statement of activities for fiscal 20X2. Such amount is paid to the Organization over a period of months and is expected to be fully paid in fiscal 20X3. The $834,413 reflected in the statement of financial position at September 30, 20X2 as contributions receivable from the United Way represents that portion of the $2,697,764 above which is unpaid at that date.

Note X: State Grant

The Association received an allocation from [*State*] under the [*Program*]. The purpose of these funds is to provide to pupils attending eligible nonpublic schools certain materials and auxiliary services routinely made available to students in public schools. The value of such allocations, $48,115 for 20X2 and $43,303 for 20X1, has been included in the Statement of Activity as both support and an expense.

The actual purchase of such materials is made by the [*Public School District*]. The School District deducts a fee equal to 4% of the allocation to offset related administrative, accounting, and handling service costs. Items purchased remain the property of the School District.

The Association also received a grant from [*State*] of $8,758 ($10,732 in 20X1) to partly defray administrative costs related to the prior school year. These grants are recorded as other support and revenues when received because it is not possible to estimate the amount of the grant from year to year.

. . . .

Note X: Research Grants and Contract Revenues [*portion of Accounting Policies note*]

Revenues from grants and contracts are recognized according to the specific agreement. Generally, revenues from restricted grants are recognized in the period of the grant award while revenues from cost reimbursement contracts are recognized to the extent of project expenses incurred. Grants and contracts are subject to audit by the awarding agency. At December 31, 20X2, the Institute has conditional grants and contracts aggregating approximately $7,600,362, which will be recognized as revenues as related project expenses are incurred.

PASS-THROUGH GIFTS (FASB STATEMENT NO. 136) [*See also Appendix D*]

Certain organizations, such as community foundations, conduct fund-raising campaigns to raise funds for other (member) agencies. The amounts raised are usually distributed to the participating agencies based upon a pre-determined formula. However, as part of the campaign, the foundation might receive contributions designated for one or more specified agencies. These should be accounted for as agency transactions, that is, a liability to the designated agency should be recorded using the guidance provided in FASB Statement No. 136, *Transfers of Assets to a Not-for-Profit Organization or Charitable Trust that Raises or Holds Contributions.* However, if the donor grants the foundation variance power, that is, the unilateral ability to override the donor's designation, the transaction should be treated as a contribution.

[*Portions of Accounting Policies notes*]

Campaign Funds Payable to Member Agencies

Pledges that are designated by donors to one or more of [*Organization's*] member agencies are recorded as campaign funds payable to member agencies. Cash received from campaigns is allocated to each participating member agency in the ratio of designated pledges from the relevant campaign, together with the pro rata share of undesignated pledges, to the total cash received. Prior to the monthly distribution of the campaign receipts to the member agencies, Board-approved expenses are deducted and recorded as administrative charges for raising funds on behalf of others.

Organization Purpose

The Campaign collects voluntary contributions and distributes them to its federated groups and other charitable organizations in accordance with donor designations. In accordance with the rules and regulations of the Campaign, undesignated contributions are allocated to the XXX Activities Programs up to X% of gross pledges. All expenses are charged to each federated group and charitable organization in proportion to their share of support from the Campaign.

Agency Transactions

As part of its annual fund-raising campaign, the Organization receives gifts that the donor designates for another entity. These are considered agency transactions, not contributions to the Organization. The organization recognizes a liability to the designated beneficiary of the gift. However, if the gift is of a nonfinancial asset, for example, equipment, it is the Organization's policy not to recognize the liability.

....

[*Separate note*]

Note X: Amounts Raised in Campaigns

Public support on the statement of activities is presented net of estimated campaign expenses and shrinkage of the campaigns. [*Organization*] includes funds raised in campaigns that distribute directly to its member agencies if [*Organization*] has had substantial involvement in that campaign. The table below presents gross pledges raised by [*Organization*] and the reconciliation to net amounts raised in campaigns.

Gross pledges	$ 15,149,789
Shrinkage	(732,028)
Campaign expenses	(1,202,931)
Net pledges	$ 13,214,830

Balance Sheet [*portion*]

Assets	
Pledges receivable (net of allowance for uncollectible pledges of $882,323)	9,292,740
Other assets	—
Liabilities	
Campaign funds payable to member agencies	10,652,647
Other liabilities	—

....

Statements of Activities [*portions*]

Changes in Unrestricted Net Assets

Amounts Raised in Campaigns (Net of campaign expenses and shrinkage—see Note X)

Campaign No. 1	$ 6,104,352
Campaign No. 2	1,594,976
State campaigns	2,963,224
Local campaigns	717,359
Private campaigns	1,834,919
Total net amounts raised in campaigns	13,214,830
Less amounts raised on behalf of others	12,521,637
Public support designated to [*Organization*]	693,193

Revenue, Gains, and Other Support

Administrative charges for raising funds on behalf of others	2,462,519

·······················

Net campaign results and revenues	
Campaign results:	
Pledges	$10,143,374
Less: uncollectible pledges	(1,264,000)
Net campaign results	8,879,374
Amounts distributed to participating agencies in accordance with donor designations	7,794,355
Amounts withheld to cover operating expenses	1,085,019
Revenues:	
Interest	14,335
Total support and revenue	1,099,354

·······················

Note X: Funds Held on Behalf of PQR Home and PQR Housing

The sole purpose of PQR Foundation is to provide support to PQR Home and PQR Housing Corp. In accordance with FASB Statement No. 136, *Transfers of Assets to a Not-for-Profit Organization or Charitable Trust that Raises or Holds Contributions for Others,* the Foundation has recorded as a liability those contributions being held on behalf of PQR Home and PQR Housing Corp.

CHALLENGE GRANTS, OTHER CONDITIONAL PROMISES TO GIVE, AND INTENTIONS TO GIVE

Note X: Conditional Promise to Give

At June 30, 20X2, the Organization had a conditional matching promise to give of $4,704,699 benefiting the [*Program*]. If matching funds of that amount are raised by December 31, 20X2, the Organization will receive forgiveness of notes payable of $3,136,466 and cash contributions of $1,568,233. The Organization has raised $3.1 million in cash from private and internal sources and another $600,000 in promises to give, and expects the entire match to be completed and verified by December 31, 20X2.

. . . .

Note X: Contracts and Grants

The University has been awarded approximately $9,900,000 in contracts and grants at September 30, 20X2, which have not been received or expended. These awards, which represent commitments of sponsors to provide funds on a cost-reimbursement basis for research and training projects, will not be reflected in the financial statements until reimbursable activities have been conducted in accordance with the provisions of the grants.

. . . .

Note X: Federal Grants

The Museum was awarded a grant of $900,000 under the National Endowment for the Humanities (NEH) Challenge Grant Program. The award is subject to certain conditions, including availability of federal appropriations in the amount of $300,000 per year for each of three years beginning October 1, 20X2 and matching by the Museum, in the ratio of 1:3 by nonfederal contributions.

To date the Museum has raised approximately $870,000, including pledges but excluding the NEH grant, in connection with this fund-raising effort. Management anticipates that sufficient funds will be raised to satisfy the full 1:3 match condition of the NEH grant.

. . . .

Note X: National Endowment for the Humanities

During fiscal 20X1, the College received approval for an $800,000 challenge grant from the National Endowment for the Humanities (NEH). The grant will be used to establish perpetual endowments for the College's humanities programs, specifically in scholarships ($300,000), faculty ($300,000), and library ($200,000).

NEH will fund $200,000, which is contingent on funding by Congress, and the College is required to raise matching funds of $600,000 over a three-year period which commenced October 1, 20X1. The College's matching funds must include cash contributions of at least $200,000; the remaining $400,000 may include cash contributions or contributions other than cash.

At June 30, 20X2, the College has raised $161,331 in cash contributions. In anticipation of successfully meeting subsequent fund-raising requirements and future funding by Congress, such amounts have been recorded in a separate fund in the permanently restricted class of net assets.

....

Note X: Challenge Grant

In 20X1, the Museum was awarded a $500,000 grant by the National Endowment for the Arts (NEA) to assist in the establishment of a 10-year term endowment for the fine arts exhibitions ($300,000) and to create a 10-year working capital reserve ($200,000). Under the terms of the grant, the Museum must meet certain terms and conditions by June 30, 20X3, including the collection of $1,500,000 of eligible matching contributions designated for the fine arts endowment fund. As of June 30, 20X2, the eligible matching amounts are reflected in the financial statements as follows:

Collected	$ 400,000
Contributions receivable, from living donors	180,000
Bequests, from estates in the process of settlement	620,000
Total	$1,200,000

....

Note X: Third-Party Reimbursement Arrangement

The Organization receives a substantial portion of its revenues from [*State*] under a grant with the State's Department of Community Affairs. This grant is renewed on an annual basis with the level of funding determined annually. Revenue is recognized on a reimbursement basis only to the extent of allowable expenses incurred. The grant requires both in-kind and cash matches as follows:

Grant Period	Grant	Cash Match	In-Kind Match
11-1-X1 to 10-31-X2	[*grant number*]	$ 6,846	$ 40,200
10-1-X2 to 9-30-X3	[*grant number*]	$ 7,218	$ 42,480

The Organization met its cash match and met its in-kind match through the contribution of fruit and vegetables from [*State*] Farm Share and from services contributed by law students. These in-kind contributions were not recorded in the accompanying financial statements because, as pass-through gifts, they did not meet the recognition criteria of generally accepted accounting principles; however, they meet the requirements for in-kind match for the Organization's grant with the Department of Community Affairs.

....

Note X: Bequests

The Organization has also been named beneficiary in a number of bequests. These gifts have not been recorded in the accompanying financial statements because the donors' wills have not yet been declared valid by the probate court and the value of the amounts to be received is not yet determinable.

Organization officials believe that the fair market value of assets to be received could be as much as $3,300,000.

. . . .

Note X: Endowment Challenge Grant

During fiscal 20X1, the Museum was awarded an $800,000 endowment challenge grant by the National Endowment for the Arts (NEA). This three-to-one challenge grant requires the Museum to generate additional endowment funds of $2,400,000, while maintaining a base-year level of operating support, as defined, during the grant period (September 1, 20X1 through June 30, 20X5).

As of June 30, 20X2, the Museum has received matching endowment gifts and pledges scheduled for payment during the grant period aggregating $1,847,687, and has more than maintained the required base level of operating support to date.

. . . .

Note X: Testamentary Gift

In February of 20W8, the Organization was notified of a gift through an estate. The gifted assets were placed in trust by the estate to be held while administration of the estate is completed. The assets consist primarily of common stock with a market value of $12,473,919 at the effective date of the gift, November 16, 20W9. As of August 31, 20X2 and 20X1, the estate has released approximately 75% of the assets of the trust. A portion of the released assets ($5,200,000 of common stock) was used to fund the frozen Musicians' Pension Plan as discussed in Note [*number*]. The estate has provided for certain contingencies in its initial allocation of assets to the trust. However, the amount of the remaining distributions from the trust may be adjusted for any cost of estate administration in excess of the amounts estimated. Remaining distributions are expected in December 20X3. The Organization recorded the estimated fair value of this contribution in fiscal 20X1 in the unrestricted Board-Designated Fund.

. . . .

Note X: Capital Contributions Received

The Organization was named as a beneficiary in the will of the late [*Donor*]. Pursuant to the will, certain assets of the estate are to be contributed to the

Organization as permanent endowment, providing that such contribution qualifies for a charitable deduction on the estate tax return filed with the Internal Revenue Service. In 20X2, even though the audit of the estate tax return was not complete, the Organization requested that the Court require that the personal representative of the Estate make a partial distribution of estate assets to the Organization. To accomplish this transfer the Organization entered into agreements with the personal representatives of the Estate and the Trustees of the [*Donor*] Trust. The agreements stipulate the assets were to be distributed to an escrow account and that the Organization could buy and sell securities held in escrow providing the principal balance originally received from the estate is left in the escrow account. The income earned from the assets held in escrow can be transferred to the operating accounts of the Organization and will become the unrestricted asset of the Organization. Also see Note [*number*]: Contingencies.

In connection with the agreements, partial distribution of assets of the [*Donor*] Trust and Estate was made on February 22, 20X2. This distribution has been recorded as permanently restricted revenue at the fair market value of the assets of $27,664,000 on that date. In addition, estimated future distributions of $15,000,000 are included in bequests receivable.

[*Additional disclosure regarding this matter is included under a separate note, Contingencies, as in the following example.*]

As disclosed in Note X, [*brief summary of facts*]. Should the Internal Revenue Service determine that the contribution of these assets to the Organization does not qualify as a charitable contribution, the Organization will be required to return the principal balance of the assets held in escrow to the Estate for redistribution to a qualified charitable organization. Accordingly, these assets have been classified as restricted assets in the balance sheet. The Organization believes the likelihood of these assets being returned to the Estate is remote.

CONTRIBUTIONS OTHER THAN CASH AND MARKETABLE SECURITIES

Note X: Contributions

Contributions of services are recognized when they are received if the services (a) create or enhance nonfinancial assets or (b) require specialized skills, are provided by individuals possessing those skills, and would typically need to be purchased if not donated. During 20X2, the value of contributed services recognized as revenues in the accompanying Statement of Activity and Changes in Net Assets was $308,000 and included consulting, legal, travel, and computer-related services.

In-kind contributions consist of donated computer system equipment and services associated with the installation of the equipment. The estimated fair value of these donations was $109,260 and $117,110 for the years ended

January 31, 20X2 and 20X1, respectively, and they are reflected as revenues in the accompanying Statement of Activity and Changes in Net Assets.

....

Note X: In-Kind Services and Materials

Contributed services of clinic personnel and medical supplies of $718,000 and $263,000 have been reflected in the financial statements as in-kind contributions during 20X2 and 20X1, respectively. Additionally, a substantial number of volunteers have donated significant amounts of time to the [*Organization*] in various capacities. However, these services have not been recognized, inasmuch as such services either do not require specialized skills or would not typically be purchased had they not been provided by donation. The value of these services is not readily determinable.

....

Note X: Contributed Services

Contributed services of professional carpenters, singers, and orchestral players are recognized as in-kind revenues at their estimated fair value when they create or enhance nonfinancial assets or they require specialized skills which would need to be purchased if they were not donated; these amounted to approximately $35,200 for 20X2 and $31,250 in 20X1.

Over 770 people participated in the Center's volunteer program during the fiscal year ended September 30, 20X2 (740 in 20X1). Community members volunteered as ushers, house managers, tour guides, administrative assistants, advisors, and trustees. A dollar valuation of their effort is not reflected in the financial statements since it does not meet the criteria for recognition. However, volunteer hours for the years ended September 30 were approximately as follows:

	20X2	20X1
Total volunteer hours	89,370	72,600

....

Note X: Contributed Services

Volunteer services have been performed by a substantial number of scientific peer reviewers who have contributed significant amounts of their time to the Organization. The Organization has valued and recorded these contributed services, which are necessary for it to carry out its programs. The Organization's management estimates that approximately 55,000 hours have been contributed by scientific peer reviewers and has valued such services at approximately $4,264,000.

....

Note X: Donations-in-Kind and Contributed Services

Material gifts-in-kind items used in the Organization's program (for example vehicle, free rent, equipment, and so on) and donated goods distributed (clothing, furniture, foodstuffs, and so on) are recorded as income and expense at the time the items are received, which is normally also the time they are placed into service or distributed.

Goods donated for sale in the Organization's thrift stores are recorded as contributions and processed donations-in-kind on the basis of a percentage of sales income determined by appraisal studies.

Contributed land, buildings, and equipment are recorded at fair value at the date of donation as unrestricted support and revenue unless the use of such contributed assets is limited by a donor-imposed restriction.

Contributed services are reported as contributions at their fair value if such services create or enhance nonfinancial assets, or would have been purchased if not provided by donation, require specialized skills, and are provided by individuals possessing such specialized skills.

....

Note X: Gifts-in-Kind

During 20X2 [*Organization*] received medical goods and supplies, with an estimated fair value of $3,882,000, to be distributed in Russia. The materials had been donated to another U.S. charity that facilitated the distribution of those goods through [*Organization*] acting as an agent. Accordingly, these have not been recognized as revenues or expenses of [*Organization*].

SPLIT-INTEREST AGREEMENTS, INCLUDING RELATED ASSETS AND LIABILITIES

See Chapter 6 of the AICPA Audit and Accounting Guide *Not-for-Profit Organizations* for further discussion of this topic.

Note X: Split-Interest Agreements

The University's split-interest agreements with donors consist primarily of charitable gift annuities, pooled income funds, and irrevocable charitable remainder trusts for which the University serves as trustee. Assets are invested and payments are made to donors and/or other beneficiaries in accordance with the respective agreements.

Contribution revenue for charitable gift annuities and charitable remainder trusts is recognized at the date the agreement is established, net of the liability recorded for the present value of the estimated future payments to be made to the respective donors and/or other beneficiaries. Contribution revenue for pooled income funds is recognized upon establishment of the agreement, at the fair value of the estimated future receipts discounted for the estimated time period to complete the agreement.

The present value of payments to beneficiaries of charitable gift annuities and charitable remainder trusts and the estimated future receipts from pooled income funds are calculated using discount rates which represent the risk-free rates in existence at the date of the gift. Gains or losses resulting from changes in actuarial assumptions and accretions of the discount are recorded as increases or decreases in the respective net asset class in the Statement of Activities.

....

Note X: Split-Interest Agreements

The Organization's investments include deferred giving vehicles subject to split-interest agreements. Three different types of agreements are currently maintained: Charitable Gift Annuity, Charitable Remainder Unitrust, and Pooled Income Fund.

Charitable Gift Annuities are unrestricted irrevocable gifts under which the Organization agrees in turn to pay a life annuity to the donor or designated beneficiary. The contributed funds and the attendant liabilities immediately become part of the general assets and liabilities of the organization, subject to the Organization's maintaining an actuarial reserve in accordance with [*State*] law. Charitable Remainder Unitrust gifts are time-restricted contributions not available to the organization until after the death of the donor, who, while living, receives an annual payout from the Trust based on a fixed percentage of the market value of the invested funds on December 31 of each year. The Pooled Income Fund comprises donations which are combined in bond and equity mutual fund investments. Contributors receive a pro rata share of the actual ordinary income of the fund until their death, at which point the investment asset share of the donors becomes available to the organization.

The Organization initially values deferred gifts of cash at face value and those of equities at market value; these values are then actuarially discounted. Published IRS discount rates are employed to determine the net present value of both contributions and liabilities pertaining to these deferred giving arrangements.

Of the $26,775,000 recorded as Investments in the Statement of Financial Position, approximately $3,795,000 represents split-interest agreements. The associated liabilities total approximately $1,955,000.

....

Note X: Charitable Lead Trusts Receivable

The Organization is the beneficiary of the income from two charitable lead trusts that it does not administer. The present value of income to be received in future years is recorded as charitable lead trusts receivable. As of December 31, 20X2, the present value of principal and imputed interest at approximately 6% to be received through the year 20Y6 is as follows:

Years Ending December 31,	Present Value	Imputed Interest	Total Income Receivable
20X3	$107,139	$ 46,963	$ 154,102
20X4	100,726	53,376	154,102
20X5	94,697	59,405	154,102
20X6	89,029	65,073	154,102
20X7–20Y6	596,287	790,916	1,387,203
	$987,878	$ 1,015,733	$ 2,003,611

....

Note X: Beneficial Interest in Trusts

The Organization receives contributions of property in which the donor or donor-designated beneficiary may retain a life interest. The assets are invested and administered by a trustee and distributions are made to the beneficiaries during the term of the agreement. These funds are invested in debt and equity securities and the Organization records its interest in these trusts at fair value based on estimated future cash receipts discounted at 5%, which approximates the Organization's rate of return on U.S. government securities. Initial recognition and subsequent adjustments to the assets' carrying value are recognized as contribution revenue and changes in value of split-interest agreements, respectively, and are classified as permanently restricted, temporarily restricted, or unrestricted support, depending on donor-imposed purpose and time restrictions, if any.

....

Note X: Annuities Payable

The Organization has received an annuity gift whereby the donors have contributed assets to the Organization in exchange for the right to receive a fixed dollar annual return during their lifetimes. A portion of the transfer is considered to be a charitable contribution for income tax purposes.

The fair value of the annuity gift over the present value of the liability for future payments, determined on an actuarial basis, has been recognized as a restricted contribution at the date of the gift. When the terms of the annuity gift have been met, the remaining amount of the gift may be reclassified to unrestricted net assets.

The assets and corresponding liabilities (including payments currently due and the present value of the estimated future actuarial liability to annuitants) of the gift annuity at June 30, 20X2 are as follows:

	Amount
Investments	$ 103,074
Annuity payable:	
Current	(8,620)
Long-term	(53,458)

·························

Note X: Annuities Payable

[*Organization*] has established a gift annuity program whereby donors may contribute assets to [*Organization*] in exchange for the right to receive a fixed-dollar annual return during their lifetime. A portion of the transfer is considered to be a charitable contribution for income tax purposes. The difference between the amount provided for the gift annuity and the present value of the liability for future payments, determined on an actuarial basis, is recognized as an unrestricted contribution at the date of the gift.

The annuity liability is revalued annually based upon actuarially computed present values. The resulting actuarial gain (loss) is recorded as other unrestricted revenue.

Change in actuarial liability consists of:

	Years Ended December 31,	
	20X2	*20X1*
Actuarial change	3,324	7,387
Annuity payments	(59,029)	(54,278)
New annuity agreements written	12,000	0
	$ (43,705)	$ (46,891)

·························

Note X: Annuities Payable

As part of certain donors' planned contributions, the Foundation has entered into charitable gift annuity contracts whereby donors contribute assets in exchange for a guaranteed fixed-dollar annual return during the lifetimes of the donors or their designees. The Foundation uses published mortality-rate tables adopted by the United States Internal Revenue Service and an assumed rate of return of approximately 6% to 8% to determine the present value of the actuarially determined liability.

·························

Note X: Pooled Income Fund

[*Organization's*] Pooled Income Fund was established in February 20W8 and is administered by [*Bank*] as the Trustee. Assets donated to the trust by a donor provide income to the donor for the remainder of the donor's life and, upon the death of the donor, the asset is transferred to the Organization subject to donor restrictions. The amounts recorded reflect the fair value of the asset, net of the present value of the estimated future payments based upon the donor's life expectancy.

EARNED INCOME AND DEFERRED REVENUE

See Chapter 6 for items related to investment income and gains.

Note X: Exchange Transactions

Exchange transactions are reciprocal transfers in which each party receives and sacrifices something of equal value, as opposed to a nonreciprocal transaction (that is, a contribution) in which a donor provides resources to support the Organization's mission and expects to receive nothing of direct value in exchange. Costs related to exchange transactions that benefit the Organization or the beneficiaries of the Organization's programs are included with the Organization's program or supporting service expenses. Costs of exchange transactions which benefit only the recipient of the exchange and not the Organization's programs or service beneficiaries are reported separately as expenses related to exchange transactions.

For the fiscal year ended August 31, 20X2, the Organization reported the following exchange transactions:

Benefits Purchased by Donors at Special Events

The Organization conducts special events in which a portion of the gross proceeds paid by the participant represents payment for the direct cost of the benefits received by the participant at the event. Unless a verifiable, objective means exists to demonstrate otherwise, the fair value of meals and entertainment provided at special events is measured at the actual cost to the Organization. The direct costs of the special events which ultimately benefit the donor rather than the Organization are recorded as exchange transaction revenue and exchange transaction expense. All proceeds received in excess of the direct costs are recorded as special events support in the accompanying combined statement of activities. In fiscal 20X2, the Organization reported special events support of approximately $106,184,000 and exchange transaction revenue and exchange transaction expense of approximately $31,198,000.

Sales of Donated Merchandise

The Organization operates [*Thrift Shop*] and [*Program*] where donations of used clothing, automobiles, and other merchandise are solicited from the public. The Organization sells this donated merchandise to generate cash, which can then be used to support the Organization's programs. In fiscal 20X2, the Organization recorded approximately $16,618,000 as merchandise and other in-kind contributions in the accompanying combined statement of activities. Sales and the corresponding cost of sales of contributed merchandise of $14,813,000 were recorded as exchange transaction revenue and exchange transaction expense. Selling and administration expenses incurred to operate the [*Thrift Shop*] and [*Program*] of $9,374,000 were also recorded as exchange transaction expense. Proceeds realized for use in the Organization's programs from these activities were $5,439,000.

Other Exchange Transactions

Other exchange transaction revenues and expenses for fiscal year 20X2 are as follows:

	Revenues	*Expenses*
Sales to third parties	$ 411,000	$ 250,000
Rental income	1,229,000	439,000
Program services fees	452,000	618,000
Royalties	3,674,000	197,000
	$ 5,766,000	$1,504,000

....

Note X: Tuition and Fees

The University maintains a policy of offering qualified applicants admission to the University without regard to financial circumstances. This policy provides for financial aid to those admitted in the form of direct grants, loans, and employment during the academic year. Tuition and fees have been reduced by certain direct grants in the amount of $25,667,000 in 20X2. In addition, the University has granted tuition reductions totaling $450,000 as part of faculty compensation in 20X2; these reductions are included in salary and benefits expense.

Admission procedures require a major portion of tuition and other charges for the entire school year to be paid by the students during the month of August, prior to opening of school. Uncollected tuition charges are reflected in the accompanying balance sheets as accounts receivable. All such receivables are considered fully collectible; accordingly, no allowance for uncollectible amounts has been provided.

....

Note X: Tuition Revenue Recognition

Revenues from tuition and fees are reported in the fiscal year in which educational programs are predominantly conducted. Fall quarter tuition and fees, collected in the prior fiscal year, are reported as deferred revenue at June 30 of each year.

....

Note X: Magazine Subscriptions

Subscription revenue is recognized over the term of the subscription. The portion applicable to subsequent years is reported as deferred revenue.

....

Note X: Membership Dues and Unearned Dues Revenue

Membership dues are assessed on a calendar year basis. Dues collected for the subsequent membership year are presented as unearned dues revenue. Life membership dues are amortized over the expected period of life members' participation in club activities. Initiation fees are recorded as income when an individual is accepted as a member.

....

Note X: Operating Revenues and Expenses

Operating revenues. Ticket sales are recorded as box office revenue on a specific performance basis. Advance ticket sales representing the receipt of payments for subscription ticket sales for the next opera season are recorded as deferred revenue in the balance sheet and are recorded as revenue as specific performances are presented.

Operating expenses. In accordance with policies generally followed by performing arts organizations, costumes and scenery for recurring productions are charged to expense when incurred.

Production costs (labor and materials) relating to future new productions are deferred until the year in which the production is presented.

Direct response marketing expenses related to the subscription campaign for the following season are deferred and recognized in the season when the related revenues are recognized; $2,625,000 and $2,437,000 of such expenses were reported as assets at July 31, 20X2 and 20X1, respectively. Other marketing costs are expensed when the advertising first takes place. Total marketing expense recognized was $9,350,000 and $8,994,000 in 20X2 and 20X1, respectively.

....

Note that the practice of recognizing all revenue for a subscription season—the same would apply to a summer school at a college—in the fiscal year in which the "majority of the performances occur" would be acceptable only if it is a large majority, so the distortion is small. If the fiscal year end falls closer to the middle of the season, the revenue should be appropriately prorated into each year.

Note X: Deferred Show Costs and Revenues

Revenues and expenses related to performances are recognized during the fiscal year in which the majority of the performances for the particular show or series occur. Annually, certain shows and series begin during the September prior to the fiscal year in which they are recognized. However, losses incurred on such shows and series prior to the end of the fiscal year are recognized when incurred.

Revenues received and expenses incurred for performances occurring in the subsequent fiscal year are deferred in the accompanying statements of financial position and included in future performance receipts and prepaid expenses, respectively. However, advertising costs are not deferred unless they are direct-response advertising that result in future benefits. The Center expenses the production costs of advertising the first time the advertising takes place, except for direct-response advertising, which is capitalized and expensed when the future benefit is realized (when the show occurs); $675,000 and $407,000 of such expenses were reported as assets at September 30, 20X2 and 20X1, respectively. Other costs are expensed when the advertising first takes place. Total advertising expense recognized was $3,250,000 and $3,194,000 in 20X2 and 20X1, respectively.

....

Note X: Operating Revenues and Expenses

Operating revenues and expenses are presented in the statement of activity on a functional basis, classified according to the significant program activity related to the purpose for which the Association exists or supporting service.

The significant activities are:

Opera Activities

Represents revenues and expenses directly associated with the production and presentation of opera performances together with production costs (labor and materials) related to new operas to be presented in future periods.

Other Presentations

Represents revenues and expenses directly associated with the presentation of attractions other than opera, where the Association either presents the attractions or leases the Opera House to third parties.

The significant supporting services are:

Opera House

Represents expenses directly associated with managing and operating the Opera House at [*Center*].

General Management

Represents expenses directly related to the overall operation of the organization which are not associated with any single program or other operating service.

Fund Raising

Represents expenses directly associated with the solicitation of contributions for the Association.

· ·

Note X: Sponsored Programs

The University receives grant and contract revenues from governmental and private sources. In 20X2, grant and contract revenues received from governmental sources totaled $237,815,000. The University recognizes revenues associated with the direct costs of sponsored programs as the related costs are incurred. Indirect costs recovered on federally sponsored programs are based on cost reimbursement rates negotiated with the University's cognizant agency, the Department of Health and Human Services (DHHS). Indirect costs recovered on all other grants and contracts are based on rates negotiated with the respective party.

· ·

Note X: Earned Revenue

Revenue from government grant and contract agreements is recognized as it is earned through expenditure in accordance with the agreements.

Revenue from program service fees is recognized when the service is completed.

· ·

Note X: Merchandising Income

Net merchandising income was derived as follows for the year ended September 30, 20X2:

Sales	$11,389,827
Less cost of goods sold	(6,487,363)
Gross profit	4,902,464
Less merchandising expenses	(3,625,049)
Net merchandising income	$ 1,277,415

EXPENSES

See additional expense-related disclosures in the "Earned Income and Deferred Revenue" section, above.

Note X: Functional Allocation of Expenses

The costs of providing museum programs and other activities have been summarized in the accompanying statement of activities. Museum programs include costs of the exhibitions and projects, curatorial activities, public service and education, and visitor services. Membership expenses represent costs associated with provision of substantive benefits to individual members. Costs associated with corporate memberships are included in fundraising expenses. Also included in fundraising expenses are costs related to the capital campaign, development, and other fundraising efforts. Management and general expenses include executive, financial administration, information systems, and personnel expenses. Rent, building maintenance, and security expenses are allocated among the functional expense categories based on staffing and space usage information.

....

Note X: Allocation of Certain Expenses

The Statement of Activities presents expenses by functional classification. Operation and maintenance of plant and depreciation are allocated based on square footage. Interest expense is allocated to the functional classifications that benefited from the use of the proceeds of the debt. Payments to affiliated organizations are allocated to functional classifications to the extent it is practicable to do so; payments which cannot be allocated are reported in the supporting service category as "unallocated payments to affiliated organizations."

....

Note X: Allocation of Joint Costs

[*Organization*] conducted activities which incurred joint costs for distribution of direct-mail fund-raising appeals and educational information, home-based activities of furlough missionaries, and related supporting office staff, as follows:

	December 31, 20X2	December 31, 20X1
Costs of informational materials and activities:		
Allocated to program	$ 64,845	$ 51,270
Allocated to fund-raising	16,211	12,818
Total joint costs	$ 81,056	$ 64,088
Salaries and expenses of furlough missionaries:		
Allocated to program	$349,864	$ 392,012

| | December 31, | |
	20X2	20X1
Allocated to fund-raising	349,863	392,011
Total joint costs	$699,727	$784,023
Salaries and expenses of office staff:		
Allocated to program	$ 86,941	$ 64,896
Allocated to fund-raising	260,825	194,687
Total joint costs	$347,766	$259,583
Total joint costs allocated to program	$501,650	$508,178
Total joint costs allocated to fund-raising	$626,899	$599,516

....

Note X: Allocation of Joint Costs

In 20X2, the Organization conducted activities that included requests for contributions, as well as program and management and general components. Those activities included direct mail campaigns, special events, and a telethon. The costs of conducting those activities included a total of $310,000 of joint costs, which are not specifically attributable to particular components of the activities. Joint costs for each kind of activity were $50,000, $150,000 and $110,000, respectively. These joint costs were allocated as follows:

Fund raising	$180,000
Program A	80,000
Program B	40,000
Management and general	10,000
Total	$310,000

....

Note X: Expense Recognition

Opera production costs are reported as expenses in the fiscal year in which that opera is first performed. Opera production costs that are paid in advance of the applicable fiscal year are recorded in prepaid expense accounts, and later expensed in the applicable fiscal year.

....

FASB Statement No. 117 requires all not-for-profit organizations to present expenses by function; voluntary health and welfare organizations must also present a statement of functional expenses by natural category (see Chapter 4 of this publication). The functional expenses may be presented either in the statement of activities, in a separate statement, or in a note. If the statement of activities presents expenses by natural category, the functional expenses can be presented in a note; and vice versa. Following are examples of note presentation of natural expenses and of functional expenses.

Note X: Natural Classification of Expenses

Operating expenses incurred in the fiscal year ended June 30, 20X2, were as follows:

Salaries, wages, and benefits	$343,682
Services and professional fees	69,576
Supplies	60,928
Travel and promotion	31,316
Other expenses	20,177
Student aid	82,156
Physical plant maintenance and equipment	73,799
Interest on indebtedness	14,978
Depreciation	18,749
Total	$715,361

Note X: Functional Expenses

The Council incurred expenses in the conduct of the following functions for the year:

The Council serves as one of the State's seven local health councils. The local health councils provide leadership in their communities to address health care issues and needs.	$ 195,981
The Council provides case management, housing placement, and insurance continuation services for people with [*disease*].	733,375
The Council functions as the local agency for two health care coalitions. Their primary objective is to address the prenatal and infant care needs of all pregnant women and infants.	386,026
Other functions of the Council include administration, administration of agency arrangements, and other health planning services.	159,496
Total	$1,474,878

FASB Statement No. 136 requires that if an organization discloses a ratio of fund-raising expenses to amounts raised, it must disclose how it computes the ratio.

Note X: Fund-Raising Expense Ratio

The following presents the Organization's fund-raising expense ratio for the year ended June 30, 20X2:

Total support reported on the statement of activities	$1,085,282
Plus donor-designated gifts	227,944
Total	1,313,226
Less in-kind rent and services	(73,015)
Adjusted support	$1,240,211
Fund-raising expenses	$ 96,939
Fund-raising expense ratio	7.82%

GRANTS AWARDED TO OTHERS

See also the "Liabilities" section in Chapter 6 for examples of disclosures pertaining to the liability for unpaid grants.

Note X: Grants Awarded

Grants awarded to others are recorded as an expense and a liability when approved by the [*Governing Board*] or when the recipient fulfills the conditions of the grant.

. . . .

Note X: Grants and Awards

The Foundation accrues grants and awards not disbursed at year end but specifically committed to designated grantees for research, health education, and medical service activities to be carried out in future fiscal years.

. . . .

Note X: Grant Expenditures and Appropriations

Grant expenditures are considered incurred at the time of approval by the Board of Trustees or the President of the Foundation for payment to a specific organization. Uncommitted appropriations that have been approved by the Board of Trustees but for which the recipient organization has not yet been identified are included in Appropriated Unrestricted Net Assets.

. . . .

Note X: Grants and Awards

Grants awarded by the Foundation usually cover a period of one year and are subject to annual renewal, as defined within the grant agreement, at the option of the Board of Trustees. Unexpended amounts of such annual grants are refundable to the Foundation by the grantee. The Foundation has expressed its intention to make a continuing annual grant in the amount of $1,000,000. Since this does not constitute a promise to give, the grant is being recorded on a year-to-year basis. The grant to the [*Institute*] amounted to $1,200,000 in 20X2.

· ·

Note X: Awards and Grants

In accordance with the Organization's guidelines, it makes awards and grants for research and professional education purposes, to be disbursed in the subsequent year, equal to one-third of the shareable income, less 15% for administration, received from its affiliates during the current year. The liability and related expense for awards and grants are recognized at the time of notification and acceptance by the recipients. Recipients are required to meet certain qualifications and to provide accountability to the Organization for funds disbursed. As of June 30, 20X2, the liability for awards and grants totals $2,653,046.

The Organization's awards for research grants-in-aid, investigators, fellowships, and professional education generally cover a period of one to five years, subject to annual renewal at the option of the Organization. The liability (awards payable) is recorded on an annual basis upon notification to the recipient at the time of approval or renewal.

· ·

Note X: Start-Up Activities

The Organization will open a shelter in 20X3 to house the homeless. The Organization will rent the facility. During 20X2, certain start-up costs were incurred to get the shelter ready to open. These costs included salaries and related costs, staff recruiting and training, rent, security, insurance, utilities, and consulting fees. These costs have been recorded as expenses in 20X2.

TAXES AND TAX-EXEMPT STATUS

See also Chapter 5 under "Contingencies and Other Uncertainties, Including Going Concern Questions."

Note X: Tax-Exempt Status

The Organization has received notification that it qualifies as a tax-exempt organization under Section 501(c)(3) of the U.S. Internal Revenue Code and corresponding provisions of [State] law and, accordingly, is not subject to federal or state income taxes.

· ·

Note X: Tax Status

The Organization is a nonprofit voluntary health agency exempt from income tax under Section 501(c)(3) of the U.S. Internal Revenue Code. The Organization has been classified as an organization that is not a private foundation and has been designated as a "publicly supported" organization. The Organization prepares separate Internal Revenue Service Forms 990 for the National Office and for the Foundation, and a combined Form 990 for the Divisions.

....

Note X: Federal Income Taxes

Under an advance ruling dated [*date*], the Internal Revenue Service ruled that the Organization will be treated as a tax-exempt, publicly supported organization under Section 501(c)(3) of the Internal Revenue Code until [*date*]. At that time the Organization will be required to submit the information to the Internal Revenue Service demonstrating that it has met the requirements of the applicable regulations during the advance ruling period. If these regulations have been met, the Organization will continue to be treated as a publicly supported organization. Management believes these regulations are being complied with.

....

Private foundations are subject to a number of specific tax rules. Notes that address some of these rules are shown in the examples that follow.

Note X: Federal Taxes

The Foundation qualifies as a tax-exempt organization under Section 501(c)(3) of the Internal Revenue Code and is not subject to federal income taxes except for income from its unrelated business activities.

Under Section 4940 of the Internal Revenue Code, a federal excise tax of 2% is normally imposed on a private foundation's net investment income (principally interest, dividends, and net realized capital gains, less expenses incurred in the production of investment income). This tax is reduced to 1% when a foundation meets certain distribution requirements. In 20X2 and 20X1, the Foundation qualified under Section 4940(e) of the Internal Revenue Code for a reduced excise tax rate of 1%.

Deferred tax expense results from certain income items being accounted for in different time periods for financial statement purposes than for federal excise tax purposes. Appropriate provisions are made in the financial statements for deferred taxes, at a 2% rate, in recognition of these timing differences.

....

Note X: Excise Tax on Net Investment Income

Tax expense differs from amounts currently payable because certain investment income is included in the statement of activities in periods that differ from those in which it is subject to taxation. The difference between tax expense and taxes currently payable is reflected as a deferred tax liability on the statements of financial position. Deferred taxes payable as of December 31, 20X2 and 20X1 are $48,560 and $19,835, respectively. For the years ended December 31, 20X2 and 20X1, tax expense consisted of the following:

	20X2	*20X1*
Currently payable	$ 79,708	$58,811
Deferred	28,725	8,019
	$108,433	$66,830

Note X: Federal Excise Tax

The Foundation is recognized as exempt from federal income tax under Section 501(c)(3) of the Internal Revenue Code (the Code) and is classified as a private foundation as defined under Section 509(a). In accordance with the provisions of the Code, the Foundation is liable for an excise tax of 2% on net investment income as defined by the Code. Deferred excise tax arises from unrealized gains on investments, and from depreciation recognized for tax purposes on real estate investments valued at market value for financial reporting purposes.

Note X: Minimum Distribution Requirement

Certain provisions of the Internal Revenue Code require that the Foundation make cash distributions in prescribed minimum amounts each year. As of December 31, 20X2, the Foundation had distributed $1,428,928 more than the required minimum distribution. Following is a summary of the computation of the excess qualifying distributions at December 31, 20X2 that will be carried forward to 20X3.

Excess qualifying distributions carried forward from 20X1	$ 2,592,310
Qualifying distributions in 20X2	4,743,482
	7,335,792
Less: Required minimum distribution	(5,906,864)
Excess of qualifying distributions over required minimum distribution	$ 1,428,928

The tax rules applicable to clubs are somewhat different from those applicable to most other not-for-profit organizations.

Note X: Federal Income Taxes

The Club is a tax-exempt organization under Section 501(c)(7) of the Internal Revenue Code. Income derived from the use of club facilities by nonmembers and investment income are considered unrelated business income which may be subject to federal tax. No provision has been made for federal income tax for the years 20X2 and 20X1 since the Club anticipates its allowable deductions will exceed unrelated business income.

....

Note X: Tax-Exempt Status

The Club is exempt from federal income tax under Section 501(c)(7) of the Internal Revenue Code. Federal income taxes are provided only where income generated from nonmember activities results in a profit to the Club.

CHAPTER 8: Financial Statements Prepared on a Basis Other Than GAAP

Many, especially smaller, not-for-profit organizations choose to present their financial statements on a basis of accounting other than generally accepted accounting principles (GAAP), often on the basis of cash receipts and disbursements. Also, for purposes of efficiency, some organizations which prepare GAAP-basis financial statements follow certain accounting policies which differ from GAAP, where the resulting differences are considered by management and by the auditor to be immaterial. The purpose of this chapter is neither to encourage nor discourage such practices, but merely to provide examples for those organizations which will find them helpful. If cash basis statements are presented, use of titles and captions including words such as revenues and expenses may not be appropriate; words such as receipts and disbursements are preferable. See also the AICPA Audit and Accounting Guide *Not-for-Profit Organizations* (paragraphs 14.11-.12) and the AICPA publication *Preparing and Reporting on Cash- and Tax-Basis Financial Statements*, by Michael J. Ramos (1998), for further discussion.

Presented below is an example of a note used to describe a cash-basis presentation and the text of an AICPA auditing interpretation on the adequacy of disclosure in financial statements prepared on a non-GAAP basis.

Note X: Basis of Accounting

The accounts of the Organization are maintained on the cash basis [*or modified cash basis*] of accounting and, accordingly, do not include interest and dividends receivable, amortization of premiums or discounts on fixed income securities, fixed assets, accrued interest expense, or other accrued liabilities. [*Add other items as relevant.*] [*Disclosure of the dollar effect of the omissions is optional.*]

....

[*AICPA Auditing Interpretation No. 14 of AU Section 523 is reprinted below.*]

Interpretation No. 14, "Evaluating the Adequacy of Disclosure and Presentation in Financial Statements Prepared in Conformity With an Other Comprehensive Basis of Accounting (OCBOA)," of AU Section 623, *Special Reports* (AICPA, *Professional Standards*, vol. 1, AU sec. 9623.90-.95)

14. Evaluating the Adequacy of Disclosure and Presentation in Financial Statements Prepared in Conformity With an Other Comprehensive Basis of Accounting *(OCBOA)*

.90 *Question*—Section 623, *Special Reports*, paragraph .10, requires that financial statements prepared on a comprehensive basis of accounting other than generally accepted accounting principles (GAAP) include a summary of significant accounting policies that discusses the basis of presentation and describes how that basis differs from GAAP. It also states that when such financial statements contain items that are the same as, or similar to, those in statements prepared in conformity with GAAP, "similar informative disclosures are appropriate." To illustrate how to apply that statement, section 623.10 says that the disclosures for depreciation, long-term debt, and owners' equity should be "comparable to" those in financial statements prepared in conformity with GAAP. That paragraph then states that the auditor "should also consider" the need for disclosure of matters that are not specifically identified on the face of the statements, such as (*a*) related party transactions, (*b*) restrictions on assets and owners' equity, (*c*) subsequent events, and (*d*) uncertainties. How should the guidance in section 623.10 be applied in evaluating the adequacy of disclosure in financial statements prepared in conformity with an other comprehensive basis of accounting (OCBOA)?

.91 *Interpretation*—The discussion of the basis of presentation may be brief; for example: "The accompanying financial statements present financial results on the accrual basis of accounting used for federal income tax reporting." Only the primary differences from GAAP need to be described. To illustrate, assume that several items are accounted for differently than they would be under GAAP, but that only the differences in depreciation calculations are significant. In that situation, a brief description of the depreciation differences is all that would be necessary, and the remaining differences need not be described. Quantifying differences is not required.

.92 If OCBOA basis financial statements contain elements, accounts, or items for which GAAP would require disclosure, the statements should either provide the relevant disclosure that would be required for those items in a GAAP presentation or provide information that communicates the substance of that disclosure. That may result in substituting qualitative information for some of the quantitative information required for GAAP presentations. For example, disclosing the repayment terms of significant long-term borrowings may sufficiently communicate information about future principal reduction without providing the summary of principal reduction during each of the next five years that would be required for a GAAP presentation. Similarly, disclosing estimated percentages of revenues, rather than amounts that GAAP presentations would require, may sufficiently convey the significance of sales or leasing to related parties. GAAP disclosure requirements that are not relevant to the measurement of the element, account, or item need not be considered. To illustrate:

a. The fair value information that FASB Statement No. 115, *Accounting for Certain Investments in Debt and Equity Securities* [AC section I80], would require disclosing for debt and equity securities reported in GAAP presentations would not be relevant when the basis of presentation does not adjust the cost of such securities to their fair value.

b. The information based on actuarial calculations that FASB Statement No. 87, *Employers' Accounting for Pensions* [AC section P16], would require disclosing for contributions to defined benefit plans reported in GAAP presentations would not be relevant in income tax or cash basis financial statements.

.93 If GAAP sets forth requirements that apply to the presentation of financial statements, then the OCBOA financial statements should either comply with those requirements or provide information that communicates the substance of those requirements. The substance of GAAP presentation requirements may be communicated using qualitative information and without modifying the financial statement format. For example:

a. Information about the effects of accounting changes, discontinued operations, and extraordinary items could be disclosed in a note to the financial statements without following the GAAP presentation requirements in the statement of results of operations, using those terms, or disclosing net-of-tax effects.

b. Instead of showing expenses by their functional classifications, the income tax basis statement of activities of a trade organization could present expenses according to their natural classifications, and a note to the statement could use estimated percentages to communicate information about expenses incurred by the major program and supporting services. A voluntary health and welfare organization could take such an approach instead of presenting the matrix of natural and functional expense classifications that would be required for a GAAP presentation, or, if information has been gathered for the Form 990 matrix required for such organizations, it could be presented either in the from of a separate statement or in a note to the financial statements.

c. Instead of showing the amounts of, and changes in, the unrestricted and temporarily and permanently restricted classes of net assets, which would be required for a GAAP presentation, the income tax basis statement of financial position of a voluntary health and welfare organization could report total net assets or fund balances, the related statement of activities could report changes in those totals, and a note to the financial statements could provide information, using estimated or actual amounts or percentages, about the restrictions on those amounts and on any deferred restricted amounts, describe the major restrictions, and provide information about significant changes in restricted amounts.

.94 Presentations using OCBOA often include a presentation consisting entirely or mainly of cash receipts and disbursements. Such presentations need not conform with the requirements for a statement of cash flows that would be included in a GAAP presentation. While a statement of cash flows is not required, if a presentation of cash receipts and disbursements is presented in a format similar to a statement of cash flows or if the entity chooses to present such a statement, for example in a presentation on the accrual basis of accounting used for federal income tax reporting, the statement should either conform to the requirements for a GAAP presentation or communicate their substance. As an example, the statement of cash flows might disclose noncash acquisitions through captions on its face.

.95 If GAAP would require disclosure of other matters, the auditor should consider the need for that same disclosure or disclosure that communicates the substance of those requirements. Some examples are contingent liabilities, going concern considerations, and significant risks and uncertainties. However, the disclosures need not include information that is not relevant to the basis of accounting. To illustrate, the general information about the use of estimates that is required to be disclosed in GAAP presentations by Statement of Position 94-6, *Disclosure of Certain Significant Risks and Uncertainties*, would not be relevant in a presentation that has no estimates, such as one based on cash receipts and disbursements.

CHAPTER 9: Information Outside the Financial Statements

Financial Accounting Standards Board (FASB) Statement of Financial Accounting Standards No. 117, *Financial Statements of Not-for-Profit Organizations*, (footnote 6 to paragraph 27) encourages, but does not require, presentation of "information about an organization's major programs or segments," and "related non-monetary information about program inputs, outputs, and results." It acknowledges, however, that such information is generally feasible only outside the basic financial statements. Part III (Statement of Program Service Accomplishments) of IRS Form 990 also requests such information. Auditors should consider their responsibilities under Statement on Auditing Standards (SAS) No. 8, *Other Information in Documents Containing Audited Financial Statements* (AICPA, *Professional Standards*, vol. 1, AU sec. 550) when such data is included in documents containing an auditor's report.

Many not-for-profit organizations prepare annual reports which include extensive narrative descriptions of the organization's programs and achievements. Also, many foundations include in such reports detailed lists of grants awarded. Examples of such narrative descriptions and lists are available elsewhere, and are not included in this publication.

Bar charts, pie charts, and graphs are often used in connection with presentation of this kind of information.

Following are examples of some presentations of non-financial-statement information (some of it also includes selected financial data) with a numeric focus.

The following example provides program-focused information.

Report of the President [*Excerpts*]

Institutional growth is demonstrated by many of the vital statistics which tell the story of the Society's work in the year 20X2: attendance at the [*Zoo and Aquarium*] increased over 20W1 to 2,182,638 visitors (1,731,300 at the [*Zoo*] and 451,338 at the [*Aquarium*]); admissions and earned income revenues grew to $5,400,000; the circulation of the Society's magazine [*Magazine*] increased to 76,000; twenty-one new courses were added to the programs of the education department at the Zoo; and five new curatorial trainees joined the scientific staff in programs sponsored by the National Endowment for the Arts and the National Museum Act. Growth in all of these areas of program and revenue in 20X2 was the accomplishment of the Society's professional staff of 385 and part-time employees numbering 425.

20X2 Animal Propagation

Propagation of the collections continued to be the greatest source of Zoo animals. During 20X2, 253 mammals, 319 birds, and 288 reptiles were born or hatched at the Zoo. Today, for example, 72% of the entire mammal collection is captive-bred. In 20S2, 50 years ago, only 35 mammals were bred at the Zoo.

Mammal Collection, [*Zoo*] at December 31, 20X2

Order	*Families*	*Species*	*Specimens*
Marsupialia—Kangaroos, phalangers, opossums	2	6	38
Chiroptera—Bats	3	12	161+
Primates—Apes, monkeys, lemurs, marmosets, etc.	6	27	130
Rodentia—Squirrels, mice, porcupines, etc.	11	25	113+
Carnivora—Bears, raccoons, cats, dogs, others, etc.	6	29	96
Pinnipedia—Seals, sea lions, etc.	2	2	4
Proboscidea—Elephants	2	2	8
Perissodactyla—Horses, tapirs, rhinoceroses	3	6	37
Edentata—Armadillos, sloths, anteaters	2	2	3
Artiodactyla—Cattle, sheep, antelopes, camels, giraffes, deer, swine, hippopotamuses	8	33	496
Totals	45	144	1086+

In 20X2 the Department of Education developed 21 new courses, bringing to 44 the programs which the department is advertising. The staff served 4,287 students in multi-session courses, 100 teachers in zoology workshops, and 1,670 adults in continuing education classes. The instructional staff was responsible for 22,213 student hours of teaching, an increase of 11% over 20X1.

Zoo-visitor profiles have demonstrated that adults constitute the majority of zoo audiences. Therefore, the department has emphasized continuing education courses. The staff has developed popular offerings on the history of zoo medicine, animal behavior, zoo photography, and classes on zoo exhibition and design. Other new audiences include school populations of the gifted and the handicapped.

	Research Projects	*Investigator*	*20X2 Grant*
Colorado	Completion of a manuscript on the status of primates	Horace Williams	$3,350
Wisconsin/ Siberia	Partial support for continuation of Siberian crane recovery plan which is part of the U.S./Russia cooperative environmental protection program	International Crane Foundation	$6,000
U.S. Northeast	Nesting site specificity of peregrine falcons	William White	$ 200
Canada	A study of environmental factors affecting high Arctic sea ice habitat of polar bears	Sandra Jones	$3,000

· ·

The following example is from an organization whose programs are largely conducted by volunteers. In the printed report, these statistics were accompanied by pie charts showing how the volunteer hours were spent.

Statistical Highlights

	20X2	20X1	20X0
Volunteers	7,468	6,710	6,953
Volunteer hours	49,142	42,846	55,324
Volunteer hours were spent as follows—services to:			
Not-for-profit organizations	24,571	12,000	27,812
Small businesses	1,475	1,283	4,150
Individuals	23,096	29,563	23,362

• •

The following example provides general statistical and financial data.

Decade in Review
Fiscal Years Ended June 30

	20X2	20W7	20W2
Financial			
Principal sources of revenues:			
Student tuition and fees	$ 258,806,000	$ 180,260,000	$ 126,351,000
Government grants and contracts	527,189,000	409,112,000	357,732,000
Investment income and gains	691,437,000	417,780,000	401,654,000
Gifts and nongovernment grants	312,771,000	180,922,000	179,263,000
Principal purposes of expenditures:			
Instruction and departmental research	408,132,000	314,726,000	225,711,000
Organized research (direct costs)	425,223,000	355,410,000	263,772,000
Libraries	61,941,000	46,840,000	40,929,000
Student aid	65,139,000	59,092,000	39,173,000
Administration, development, and general	151,747,000	105,019,000	68,625,000
Assets:			
Investments at market	5,031,550,000	2,518,579,000	1,696,277,000
Construction in progress	107,934,000	89,100,000	81,309,000
Plant facilities net of depreciation	1,016,315,000	754,168,000	405,364,000
Other assets	1,045,006,000	1,380,432,000	945,993,000
Liabilities and net assets:			
Notes and bonds payable	729,481,000	458,175,000	331,979,000
Other liabilities	673,616,000	516,526,000	328,083,000
Total net assets	5,797,708,000	3,767,578,000	2,468,881,000

(*continued*)

	20X2	20W7	20W2
Certain financial ratios:			
Fundraising costs to funds raised	8.6%	8.8%	8.7%
Program expenses to total expenses	86.3%	84.7%	85.1%
Students			
Enrollment:			
Undergraduate	6,577	6,555	6,524
Graduate and professional	7,467	6,886	6,555
Degrees conferred:			
Bachelor degrees	1,744	1,633	1,649
Advanced degrees	2,900	2,455	2,510
Annual undergraduate tuition rate	$19,695	$14,280	$10,476
Faculty			
Members of the Academic Council	1,459	1,375	1,295

· ·

The following example provides information about investment policies.

Approved asset classes, policy targets, target ranges, and index benchmarks are as follows:

Asset Segment	Target %	Range %	Index Benchmark
U.S. core equity	25.0%	20.0-30.0	S&P 500
U.S. mid/small growth equity	7.5%	5.0-10.0	Russell Mid Growth
U.S. mid/small value equity	7.5%	5.0-10.0	Russell Mid Value
International core and emerging market equity	30.0%	25.0-35.0	EAFE/FC Index
Total equity	70.0%	65.0-75.0	Russell 3000
U.S. fixed income	15.0%	10.0-20.0	LBIG/C
Global fixed income	15.0%	10.0-20.0	JPM Global Government
Total fixed income	30.0%	25.0-35.0	
Cash equivalents and short term	0.0%	0.0-10.0	

· ·

Highlights FYX2—The Year in Review

A total of 2,329 individuals were provided skills training in seven African countries. In addition the performance records of fiscal year 20X2 include:

- 21 [*Organization*] Interest Groups being developed in 16 countries
- 4 Pre-project appraisal studies completed
- 2 Feasibility studies completed
- 10 Program proposals developed
- 1 New program in operational stage in [*Location*]

- 3 New programs being readied for start-up in [*Locations*]
- 32% of [*Organization*] budget obtained from non-U.S. government sources
- 220 Person-days of on-site technical assistance provided in eight countries
- Management and control systems strengthened in 10 programs
- Planning on-going for [*Organization's*] first African Development Conference to be held in [*Location*] in 20X3
- Potential sources of financial support such as corporations and foundations identified

....

Highlights of 20X2

[*Organization*] provides training and technical assistance to [*Third World area*] enterprises composed of large numbers of rural people. Our training helps them to increase productivity, improve their marketing, and enhance their overall management. The results of our assistance include job creation, increased levels of income for needy people, and overall improvement in living conditions, without creating dependence on outside assistance.

We currently have a staff of over 150 persons, made up primarily of highly qualified citizens of the countries where we operate. We are funded by church organizations, individuals, foundations, corporations, host country institutions, and the U.S. Agency for International Development.

In 20X2 [*Organization*] provided assistance to 260 community-based enterprises, projects, and related institutions. Over 1,000,000 men, women, and children benefited from this year's work. Annual gross revenues of the enterprises and projects we assisted were over $16,000,000, and project assets exceeded $28,000,000.

For the first time in our history, private grants and contributions for our work reached the $1 million mark. This represents nearly a 400% increase over the level of just five years ago.

....

Programs and Activities [*Excerpts*]

As of May 31, 20X2, [*Organization*] membership included 1,995 institutional members, 125 associate members, and 227 subscribers. Growth in the association is illustrated in the accompanying graph.

In 20X1-20X2, a total of 48 workshops on 16 topics were completed with 2,900 participants from 1,809 institutions attending. Volunteers included 80 faculty members, 52 planning committee members, and 40 on-site assistants. The 20X2-X3 professional development season will feature 5 brand new and 11 updated workshops....

Over 1,300 members, guests, and exhibitors met in Chicago from July 8-11 for [*Organization's*] Annual Meeting. Featured were distinguished speakers from the private and public sectors who addressed issues of concern to [*members*]. Distinguished [*Member*] Awards were presented to: ....

Two new books were published during the year: .... Production of four new books is scheduled: .... 22 news releases were sent to over 200 media sources.

APPENDIX A: Excerpts From FASB Statement of Financial Accounting Standards No. 117, *Financial Statements of Not-for-Profit Organizations**

[*Appendix C of FASB Statement No. 117 is reprinted below.*]

APPENDIX C: ILLUSTRATIVE EXAMPLES

153. This appendix provides illustrations of statements of financial position, statements of activities, and statements of cash flows. These illustrations are intended as examples only; they present only a few of the permissible formats. Other formats or levels of detail may be appropriate for certain circumstances. Organizations are encouraged to provide information in ways that are most relevant and understandable to donors, creditors, and other external users of financial statements. The Board encourages organizations to provide comparative financial statements; however, for simplicity, the illustrative statements of activities and statements of cash flows provide information for a single period.

154. The illustrations also include certain notes to the financial statements for matters discussed in this Statement. The illustrative notes are not intended to illustrate compliance with all generally accepted accounting principles and specialized accounting and reporting principles and practices.

155. Shading is used to highlight certain basic totals that must be reported in financial statements to comply with the provisions of this Statement. This Statement requires not only reporting those certain basic totals but also reporting components of those aggregates; for example, it requires reporting information about the gross amounts of items of revenues and expenses and cash receipts and payments.

Statement of Financial Position

156. A Statement of financial position that sequences assets and liabilities based on their relative liquidity is presented. For example, cash and contributions receivable restricted by donors to investment in land, buildings, and equipment are not included with the line items "cash and cash equivalents" or "contributions receivable." Rather, those items are reported as "assets restricted

* FASB Statement No. 117, *Financial Statements of Not-for-Profit Organizations*, is copyrighted by the Financial Accounting Standards Board, 401 Merritt 7, P.O. Box 5116, Norwalk, Connecticut 06856-5116, U.S.A. Portions are reprinted with permission. Complete copies of this document are available from the FASB.

to investment in land, buildings, and equipment" and are sequenced closer to "land, buildings, and equipment"; cash and cash equivalents of permanent endowment funds held temporarily until suitable long-term investment opportunities are identified are included in the classification "long-term investments." Assets and liabilities also may be arrayed by their relationship to net asset classes, classified as current and noncurrent, or arranged in other ways. Comparative statements of financial position are provided to facilitate understanding of the statement of cash flows.

Not-for-Profit Organization
Statements of Financial Position
June 30, 19X1 and 19X0
(in thousands)

	19X1	19X0
Assets:		
Cash and cash equivalents	$ 75	$ 460
Accounts and interest receivable	2,130	1,670
Inventories and prepaid expenses	610	1,000
Contributions receivable	3,025	2,700
Short-term investments	1,400	1,000
Assets restricted to investment in land, buildings, and equipment	5,210	4,560
Land, buildings, and equipment	61,700	63,590
Long-term investments	218,070	203,500
Total assets	$292,220	$278,480
Liabilities and net assets:		
Accounts payable	$ 2,570	$ 1,050
Refundable advance		650
Grants payable	875	1,300
Notes payable		1,140
Annuity obligations	1,685	1,700
Long-term debt	5,500	6,500
Total liabilities	10,630	12,340
Net assets:		
Unrestricted	115,228	103,670
Temporarily restricted (Note B)	24,342	25,470
Permanently restricted (Note C)	142,020	137,000
Total net assets	281,590	266,140
Total liabilities and net assets	$292,220	$278,480

....

Note: Paragraph 100 of FASB Statement No. 117 is included here, alongside the reprint of Appendix C, for additional guidance.

100. The Board concluded that while definitions are necessary to make the distinctions required by this Statement, stringent requirements to use specific terms are not necessary to faithfully represent those distinctions. As illustrated in Appendix C, this Statement encourages the use of the terms unrestricted, temporarily restricted, and permanently restricted net assets; however, the Board knows that other labels exist. For example, *equity* may be used for net assets, and *other* or *not donor-restricted* may be used with care to distinguish unrestricted net assets from the temporarily and permanently restricted classes of net assets. For example, the net asset section might be arranged as follows:

Donor restricted:		
Permanently		$XXX
Temporarily		XXX
Other:		
Designated by the Board for [*purpose*]	$XXX	
Undesignated	<u>XXX</u>	<u>XXX</u>
Net assets		$XXX

At a minimum, the amounts for each of the three classes of net assets and the total of net assets must be reported in a statement of financial position and the captions used to describe those amounts must correspond with their meanings, as defined by this Statement. A few respondents to the Exposure Draft suggested that organizations should be required to report separate amounts of unrestricted net assets designated by the governing board for long-term investment or for investment in plant. The Board concluded that those disclosures are not essential and that organizations should be permitted but not required to provide those or other disclosures on the face of financial statements or in notes to financial statements.

Statement of Activities

157. Three formats of statements of activities are presented. Each format has certain advantages. Format A reports information in a single column. That format most easily accommodates presentation of multiyear comparative information. Format B reports the same information in columnar format with a column for each class of net assets and adds an optional total column. That format makes evident that the effects of expirations on donor restrictions result in reclassifications between classes of net assets. It also accommodates presentation of aggregated information about contributions and investment

income for the entity as a whole. Format C reports information in two statements with summary amounts from a statement of revenues, expenses, and other changes in unrestricted net assets (Part 1 of 2) articulating with a statement of changes in net assets (Part 2 of 2). Alternative formats for the statement of changes in net assets—a single column and a multicolumn—are illustrated. The two-statement approach of Format C focuses attention on changes in unrestricted net assets. That format may be preferred by organizations that view their *operating* activities as excluding receipts of donor-restricted revenues and gains from contributions and investment income. To facilitate comparison of the formats, the same level of aggregation is used in each of the statements of activities.

158. The three illustrative statements of activities show items of revenues and gains first, then expenses, then losses; reclassifications, which must be shown separately, are reported with revenues and gains. Those items could be arranged in other ways and other subtotals may be included. For example, the items may be sequenced as (a) revenues, expenses, gains and losses, and reclassifications shown last or (b) certain revenues, less directly related expenses, followed by a subtotal, then other revenues, other expenses, gains and losses, and reclassifications. Paragraph 167 provides an example that shows how items may be sequenced to distinguish between operating and nonoperating activities or to make other distinctions, if desired.

159. Although the illustrative statements of activities report by function, expenses may be reported by natural classification in the statements with functional classification disclosed in the notes.

Format A

Not-for-Profit Organization
Statement of Activities
Year Ended June 30, 19X1
(in thousands)

Changes in unrestricted net assets:	
Revenues and gains:	
Contributions	$ 8,640
Fees	5,400
Income on long-term investments (Note E)	5,600
Other investment income (Note E)	850
Net unrealized and realized gains on long-term investments (Note E)	8,228
Other	150
Total unrestricted revenues and gains	28,868
Net assets released from restrictions (Note D):	
Satisfaction of program restrictions	11,990

Satisfaction of equipment acquisition restrictions	1,500
Expiration of time restrictions	1,250
Total net assets released from restrictions	14,740
Total unrestricted revenues, gains, and other support	43,608
Expenses and losses:	
Program A	13,100
Program B	8,540
Program C	5,760
Management and general	2,420
Fund raising	2,150
Total expenses (Note F)	31,970
Fire loss	80
Total expenses and losses	32,050
Increase in unrestricted net assets	11,558
Changes in temporarily restricted net assets:	
Contributions	8,110
Income on long-term investments (Note E)	2,580
Net unrealized and realized gains on long-term investments (Note E)	2,952
Actuarial loss on annuity obligations	(30)
Net assets released from restrictions (Note D)	(14,740)
Decrease in temporarily restricted net assets	(1,128)
Changes in permanently restricted net assets:	
Contributions	280
Income on long-term investments (Note E)	120
Net unrealized and realized gains on long-term investments (Note E)	4,620
Increase in permanently restricted net assets	5,020
Increase in net assets	15,450
Net assets at beginning of year	266,140
Net assets at end of year	$281,590

Format B

Not-for-Profit Organization
Statement of Activities
Year Ended June 30, 19X1
(in thousands)

	Unrestricted	Temporarily Restricted	Permanently Restricted	Total
Revenues, gains, and other support:				
Contributions	$ 8,640	$ 8,110	$ 280	$ 17,030
Fees	5,400			5,400
Income on long-term investments (Note E)	5,600	2,580	120	8,300
Other investment income (Note E)	850			850
Net unrealized and realized gains on long-term investments (Note E)	8,228	2,952	4,620	15,800
Other	150			150
Net assets released from restrictions (Note D):				
Satisfaction of program restrictions	11,990	(11,990)		
Satisfaction of equipment acquisition restrictions	1,500	(1,500)		
Expiration of time restrictions	1,250	(1,250)		
Total revenues, gains, and other support	43,608	(1,098)	5,020	47,530
Expenses and losses:				
Program A	13,100			13,100
Program B	8,540			8,540
Program C	5,760			5,760
Management and general	2,420			2,420
Fund raising	2,150			2,150
Total expenses (Note F)	31,970			31,970
Fire loss	80			80
Actuarial loss on annuity obligations		30		30
Total expenses and losses	32,050	30		32,080
Change in net assets	11,558	(1,128)	5,020	15,450
Net assets at beginning of year	103,670	25,470	137,000	266,140
Net assets at end of year	$115,228	$24,342	$142,020	$281,590

Format C, Part 1 of 2

Not-for-Profit Organization
Statement of Unrestricted Revenues, Expenses, and
Other Changes in Unrestricted Net Assets
Year Ended June 30, 19X1
(in thousands)

Unrestricted revenues and gains:	
Contributions	$ 8,640
Fees	5,400
Income on long-term investments (Note E)	5,600
Other investment income (Note E)	850
Net unrealized and realized gains on long-term investments (Note E)	8,228
Other	150
Total unrestricted revenues and gains	28,868
Net assets released from restrictions (Note D):	
Satisfaction of program restrictions	11,990
Satisfaction of equipment acquisition restrictions	1,500
Expiration of time restrictions	1,250
Total net assets released from restrictions	14,740
Total unrestricted revenues, gains, and other support	43,608
Expenses and losses:	
Program A	13,100
Program B	8,540
Program C	5,760
Management and general	2,420
Fund raising	2,150
Total expenses (Note F)	31,970
Fire loss	80
Total unrestricted expenses and losses	32,050
Increase in unrestricted net assets	$11,558

Format C, Part 2 of 2

Not-for-Profit Organization
Statement of Changes in Net Assets
Year Ended June 30, 19X1
(in thousands)

Unrestricted net assets:	
Total unrestricted revenues and gains	$ 28,868
Net assets released from restrictions (Note D)	14,740
Total unrestricted expenses and losses	(32,050)
Increase in unrestricted net assets	11,558
Temporarily restricted net assets:	
Contributions	8,110
Income on long-term investments (Note E)	2,580
Net unrealized and realized gains on long-term investments (Note E)	2,952
Actuarial loss on annuity obligations	(30)
Net assets released from restrictions (Note D)	(14,740)
Decrease in temporarily restricted net assets	(1,128)
Permanently restricted net assets:	
Contributions	280
Income on long-term investments (Note E)	120
Net unrealized and realized gains on long-term investments (Note E)	4,620
Increase in permanently restricted net assets	5,020
Increase in net assets	15,450
Net assets at beginning of year	266,140
Net assets at end of year	$ 281,590

Format C, Part 2 of 2 (Alternate)

Not-for-Profit Organization
Statement of Changes in Net Assets
Year Ended June 30, 19X1
(in thousands)

	Unrestricted	Temporarily Restricted	Permanently Restricted	Total
Revenues, gains, and other support:				
Unrestricted revenues, gains, and other support	$ 28,868			$ 28,868
Restricted revenues, gains, and other support:				
Contributions		$ 8,110	$ 280	8,390
Income on long-term investments (Note E)		2,580	120	2,700
Net unrealized and realized gains on long-term investments (Note E)		2,952	4,620	7,572
Net assets released from restrictions (Note D)	14,740	(14,740)		
Total revenues, gains, and other support	43,608	(1,098)	5,020	47,530
Expenses and losses:				
Unrestricted expenses and losses	32,050			32,050
Actuarial loss on annuity obligations		30		30
Total expenses and losses	32,050	30		32,080
Change in net assets	11,558	(1,128)	5,020	15,450
Net assets at beginning of year	103,670	25,470	137,000	266,140
Net assets at end of year	$115,228	$ 24,342	$142,020	$281,590

Statement of Cash Flows

160. Statements of cash flows are illustrated using both the direct and indirect methods of reporting cash flow from operating activities.

Direct Method

Not-for-Profit Organization
Statement of Cash Flows
Year Ended June 30, 19X1
(in thousands)

Cash flows from operating activities:		
Cash received from service recipients	$	5,220
Cash received from contributors		8,030
Cash collected on contributions receivable		2,615
Interest and dividends received		8,570
Miscellaneous receipts		150
Interest paid		(382)
Cash paid to employees and suppliers		(23,808)
Grants paid		(425)
Net cash used by operating activities		(30)
Cash flows from investing activities:		
Insurance proceeds from fire loss on building		250
Purchase of equipment		(1,500)
Proceeds from sale of investments		76,100
Purchase of investments		(74,900)
Net cash used by investing activities		(50)
Cash flows from financing activities:		
Proceeds from contributions restricted for:		
Investment in endowment		200
Investment in term endowment		70
Investment in plant		1,210
Investment subject to annuity agreements		200
		1,680
Other financing activities:		
Interest and dividends restricted for reinvestment		300
Payments of annuity obligations		(145)
Payments on notes payable		(1,140)
Payments on long-term debt		(1,000)
		(1,985)
Net cash used by financing activities		(305)
Net decrease in cash and cash equivalents		(385)
Cash and cash equivalents at beginning of year		460
Cash and cash equivalents at end of year	$	75
Reconciliation of change in net assets to net cash used by operating activities:		
Change in net assets	$	15,450

Adjustments to reconcile change in net assets to net cash
  used by operating activities:

Depreciation	3,200
Fire loss	80
Actuarial loss on annuity obligations	30
Increase in accounts and interest receivable	(460)
Decrease in inventories and prepaid expenses	390
Increase in contributions receivable	(325)
Increase in accounts payable	1,520
Increase in refundable advance	(650)
Decrease in grants payable	(425)
Contributions restricted for long-term investment	(2,740)
Interest and dividends restricted for long-term investment	(300)
Net unrealized and realized gains on long-term investments	(15,800)
Net cash used by operating activities	$ (30)

Supplemental data for noncash investing and financing activities:

Gifts of equipment	$ 140
Gift of paid-up life insurance, cash surrender value	80

Indirect Method

Not-for-Profit Organization
Statement of Cash Flows
Year Ended June 30, 19X1
(in thousands)

Cash flows from operating activities:

Change in net assets	$ 15,450

Adjustments to reconcile change in net assets to net
  cash used by operating activities:

Depreciation	3,200
Fire loss	80
Actuarial loss on annuity obligations	30
Increase in accounts and interest receivable	(460)
Decrease in inventories and prepaid expenses	390
Increase in contributions receivable	(325)
Increase in accounts payable	1,520
Decrease in refundable advance	(650)
Decrease in grants payable	(425)
Contributions restricted for long-term investment	(2,740)
Interest and dividends restricted for long-term investment	(300)
Net unrealized and realized gains on long-term investments	(15,800)
Net cash used by operating activities	(30)

(*continued*)

Cash flows from investing activities:	
Insurance proceeds from fire loss on building	250
Purchase of equipment	(1,500)
Proceeds from sale of investments	76,100
Purchase of investments	(74,900)
Net cash used by investing activities	(50)
Cash flows from financing activities:	
Proceeds from contributions restricted for:	
Investment in endowment	200
Investment in term endowment	70
Investment in plant	1,210
Investment subject to annuity agreements	200
	1,680
Other financing activities:	
Interest and dividends restricted for reinvestment	300
Payments of annuity obligations	(145)
Payments on notes payable	(1,140)
Payments on long-term debt	(1,000)
	(1,985)
Net cash used by financing activities	(305)
Net decrease in cash and cash equivalents	(385)
Cash and cash equivalents at beginning of year	460
Cash and cash equivalents at end of year	$ 75
Supplemental data:	
Noncash investing and financing activities:	
Gifts of equipment	$ 140
Gift of paid-up life insurance, cash surrender value	80
Interest paid	382

Notes to Financial Statements

161. Illustrative Note A provides required policy disclosures (paragraphs 14 and 16 of Statement 116) that bear on the illustrated statements and Notes B and C provide information required by this Statement. Notes D through F provide information that not-for-profit organizations are encouraged to disclose. However, paragraph 26 requires voluntary health and welfare organizations to provide the information in Note F in a statement of functional expenses. All amounts are in thousands.

Note A

The Organization reports gifts of cash and other assets as restricted support if they are received with donor stipulations that limit the use of the donated assets. When a donor restriction expires, that is, when a stipulated time restriction ends or purpose restriction is accomplished, temporarily restricted net assets are reclassified to unrestricted net assets and reported in the statement of activities as net assets released from restrictions.

The Organization reports gifts of land, buildings, and equipment as unrestricted support unless explicit donor stipulations specify how the donated assets must be used. Gifts of long-lived assets with explicit restrictions that specify how the assets are to be used and gifts of cash or other assets that must be used to acquire long-lived assets are reported as restricted support. Absent explicit donor stipulations about how long those long-lived assets must be maintained, the Organization reports expirations of donor restrictions when the donated or acquired long-lived assets are placed in service.

Note B

Temporarily restricted net assets are available for the following purposes or periods:

Program A activities:	
Purchase of equipment	$ 3,060
Research	4,256
Educational seminars and publications	1,520
Program B activities:	
Disaster relief	2,240
Educational seminars and publications	2,158
Program C activities: general	2,968
Buildings and equipment	2,150
Annuity trust agreements	2,850
For periods after June 30, 20X1	3,140
	$ 24,342

Note C

Permanently restricted net assets are restricted to:

Investment in perpetuity, the income from which is expendable to support:	
Program A activities	$ 27,524
Program B activities	13,662
Program C activities	13,662
Any activities of the organization	81,972
	136,820
Endowment requiring income to be added to original gift until fund's value is $2,500	2,120
Paid-up life insurance policy that will provide proceeds upon death of insured for an endowment to support general activities	80
Land required to be used as a recreation area	3,000
	$142,020

Note D

Net assets were released from donor restrictions by incurring expenses satisfying the restricted purposes or by occurrence of other events specified by donors.

Purpose restrictions accomplished:	
Program A expenses	$ 5,800
Program B expenses	4,600
Program C expenses	1,590
	11,990
Program A equipment acquired and placed in service	1,500
Time restrictions expired:	
Passage of specified time	850
Death of annuity beneficiary	400
	1,250
Total restrictions released	$14,740

Note E

Investments are carried at market or appraised value, and realized and unrealized gains and losses are reflected in the statement of activities. The Organization invests cash in excess of daily requirements in short-term investments. At June 30, 19X1, $1,400 was invested short term, and during the year short- term investments earned $850. Most long-term investments are held in two investment pools. Pool A is for permanent endowments and the unappropriated net appreciation of those endowments. Pool B is for amounts designated by the board of trustees for long-term investment. Annuity trusts, term endowments, and certain permanent endowments are separately invested. Long-term investment activity is reflected in the table below:

	Pool A	Pool B	Other	Total
Investments at beginning of year	$164,000	$32,800	$6,700	$203,500
Gifts available for investment:				
Gifts creating permanent endowment	200	80	280	
Gifts creating term endowments		70	70	
Gifts creating annuity trusts		200	200	
Amount withdrawn at death of annuitant			(400)	(400)
Investment returns (net of expenses of $375):				
Dividends, interest, and rents	6,000	2,000	300	8,300
Realized and unrealized gains	12,000	3,800	—	15,800
Total return on investments	18,000	5,800	300	24,100
Amounts appropriated for current operations	(7,500)	(2,000)		(9,500)
Annuity trust income for current and future payments	—	—	(180)	(180)
Investments at end of year	$174,700	$ 36,600	$ 6,770	$218,070

The participation in the pools and ownership of the other investments at June 30, 19X1 is shown in the table below:

	Pool A	Pool B	Other	Total
Permanently restricted net assets	$136,820		$2,200	$139,020
Temporarily restricted net assets	10,752		4,570	15,322
Unrestricted net assets	27,128	$36,600		63,728
	$174,700	$36,600	$6,770	$218,070

The board of trustees has interpreted state law as requiring the preservation of the purchasing power (real value) of the permanent endowment funds unless explicit donor stipulations specify how net appreciation must be used. To meet that objective, the Organization's endowment management policies require that net appreciation be retained permanently in an amount necessary to adjust the historic dollar value of original endowment gifts by the change in the Consumer Price Index. After maintaining the real value of the permanent endowment funds, any remainder of total return is available for appropriation. In 19X1, the total return on Pool A was $18,000 (10.6 percent), of which $4,620 was retained permanently to preserve the real value of the original gifts. The remaining $13,380 was available for appropriation by the board of trustees. State law allows the board to appropriate so much of net appreciation as is prudent considering the Organization's long- and short-term needs, present and anticipated financial requirements, expected total return on its investments, price level trends, and general economic conditions. Under the Organization's endowment spending policy, 5 percent of the average of the market value at the end of the previous 3 years is appropriated, which was $7,500 for the year ended June 30, 19X1.

Note F

Expenses incurred were for:

	Total	Program A	Program B	Program C	Management and General	Fund Raising
Salaries, wages, and benefits	$15,115	$ 7,400	$3,900	$ 1,725	$1,130	$ 960
Grants to other organizations	4,750	2,075	750	1,925		
Supplies and travel	3,155	865	1,000	490	240	560
Services and professional fees	2,840	160	1,490	600	200	390
Office and occupancy	2,528	1,160	600	450	218	100
Depreciation	3,200	1,440	800	570	250	140
Interest	382				382	
Total expenses	$31,970	$13,100	$8,540	$5,760	$2,420	$2,150

Transactions Reported in the Illustrative Financial Statements

162. The following facts and transactions are reflected in the illustrative financial statements. The transactions are presented by class of net assets to facilitate locating their effects in the statements and notes.

The following transactions affect unrestricted net assets:

a. The organization invested cash in excess of daily requirements in short-term investment instruments. Interest earned on these investments totaled $850. The governing board has designated a portion of unrestricted net assets for long-term investment. Those assets earned $2,000.

b. The organization received unrestricted contributions of the following: cash, $5,120; recognizable contributed services, $300; other consumable assets, $1,410; equipment, $140; and unconditional promises to give to support activities of 19X1, $1,020.

c. Equipment with an original cost of $660 and accumulated depreciation of $330 was destroyed in a fire. Insurance proceeds of $250 were received. The equipment was originally purchased with unrestricted assets.

d. All conditions of a prior year's grant of $650 were substantially met. The grant proceeds were originally recorded as a refundable advance.

e. The organization made a payment of $425 on its prior year unconditional grant to an unrelated agency.

f. The organization repaid $1,140 of its notes payable. Interest of $32 was incurred and paid on these notes.

g. The organization repaid $1,000 of its long-term debt. Interest of $350 was incurred and paid on the debt.

h. Depreciation amounted to $3,200.

The following transactions affect temporarily restricted net assets:

i. The organization received temporarily restricted contributions as follows:

Restricted to	Cash	Consumable Assets	Promises to Give
Program purposes	$2,170	$ 960	$ 990
Use in future periods	740		930
Acquisition of land, buildings, and equipment	770		1,380

j. In addition, a donor transferred cash of $200 to set up an annuity trust having a related annuity obligation with a present value of $100. Upon the death of the beneficiary, the remaining interest will be used for a donor-stipulated purpose.

k. In addition, a donor contributed cash of $70 to create a term endowment. At the end of 15 years the endowment assets can be used to support the organization's operations.

l. The organization made payments of $145 to beneficiaries of annuity trust agreements.

The following transactions affect permanently restricted net assets:

m. A donor contributed a paid-up life insurance policy with a cash surrender value of $80. Upon the death of the insured, the death benefit must be used to create a permanent endowment. There was no change in the cash surrender value between the date of the gift and the end of the fiscal year.

n. A donor contributed cash of $200 to create a permanent endowment fund. The income is restricted to use for Program A activities.

The following transactions affect more than one class of net assets:

o. The organization collected promises to give of $3,055: $980 of amounts for unrestricted purposes, $610 of amounts restricted to future periods, $1,025 of amounts restricted to program purposes, and $440 of amounts for acquisition of land, buildings, and equipment.

p. The organization utilized all of the $1,410 consumable assets contributed for unrestricted purposes, and $350 of the $960 consumable assets contributed for program purposes.

q. A trust annuitant died and the $400 remainder interest became available for the unrestricted use of the organization. Management decided to invest the remainder interest in short-term investments. The actuarial gain on death of the annuitant is included in the actuarial loss on annuity obligations.

r. The organization acquired and placed in service $1,500 of equipment for Program A; temporarily restricted net assets were available at the time the equipment was purchased.

s. The net gain, unrealized and realized, on unrestricted net assets designated by the governing board for long-term investment of $3,800 was recognized. The net gain, unrealized and realized, on permanent endowments and the unappropriated net appreciation of those endowments of $12,000 was recognized. The governing board has interpreted the law in its jurisdiction as requiring preservation of purchasing power. The governing board has selected the CPI as the measure of changes in purchasing power. The CPI has changed by 3.5 percent over the year. The index-adjusted original gift amount of the endowment at the end of the previous year was $132,000.

t. The organization reinvested the yield of $120 on a permanent endowment that requires income to be added to the original gift until the fund's value is $2,500.

Statement of Activities With Additional Classifications

163. This Statement neither encourages nor discourages organizations from classifying items of revenues, expenses, and other changes in net assets as operating and nonoperating, expendable and nonexpendable, earned and unearned, recurring and nonrecurring, or in other ways. Rather, the requirements of this Statement provide a few broad constraints for a statement of activities and allow not-for-profit organizations latitude to make distinctions that they believe will provide meaningful information to users of their financial statements. Like business enterprises, that latitude allows organizations to report an undefined intermediate measure of operations. That latitude also allows reporting practices to develop in an evolutionary manner for all or certain kinds of not-for-profit organizations.

164. Entities that use terms such as *operating income, operating profit, operating surplus, operating deficit,* and *results of operations* often use those terms with different meanings. Business enterprises that choose to make an operating and nonoperating distinction do so within an income statement (statement of earnings) that at a minimum reports net income for the period as well as an intermediate measure of income before the effects of a discontinued operating segment, extraordinary items, or an accounting change, if any.

165. Paragraph 23 imposes a similar constraint on not-for-profit organizations that choose to use similar terms. If an organization reports an intermediate measure of *operations*, it must do so within a financial statement that, at a minimum, reports the change in unrestricted net assets for the period. Paragraph 23 also specifies that if an organization's use of the term *operations* is not apparent from the details provided on the face of the statement, a note to financial statements should describe the nature of the reported measure of operations or the items excluded from operations.

166. A statement of unrestricted revenues, expenses, and other changes in unrestricted net assets that subdivides all transactions and other events and circumstances to make an operating and nonoperating distinction is illustrated. This example uses part 1 of 2 of Format C of the previously illustrated statements of activities to show a measure of operations-change in unrestricted net assets from operations.

167. The shaded areas depict the constraints imposed by this Statement and by generally accepted accounting principles to report appropriately labeled subtotals for changes in classes of net assets before the effects of discontinued operating segments, extraordinary items, or accounting changes, if any. The unshaded areas depict areas within the statement for which there is latitude to sequence and classify items of revenues and expenses. Other formats also may be used. For example, the single-statement approach of Format B may be helpful in describing an organization's ongoing major or central operations if that organization's view of operating activities includes receiving donor-restricted revenues from contributions and investment income.

Other Not-for-Profit Organization
Statement of Unrestricted Revenues, Expenses, and
Other Changes in Unrestricted Net Assets
Year Ended June 30, 19X1
(in thousands)

Operating revenues and support:	
Fees from providing services	$ X,XXX
Operating support	X,XXX
Net assets released from restrictions	X,XXX
Total operating revenues and support	XX,XXX
Operating expenses:	
Programs	XX,XXX
Management and general	X,XXX
Fund raising	X,XXX
Total operating expenses	XX,XXX
Change in unrestricted net assets from operations	X,XXX
Other changes:	
[*Items considered to be nonoperating*	X,XXX
(paragraphs 65-68 and 111-115).]	X,XXX
Change in net assets before effects of discontinued operations extraordinary items, and changes in accounting principles	XX,XXX
Discontinued operations	X,XXX
Extraordinary items	X,XXX
Changes in accounting principles	X,XXX
Change in net assets	XX,XXX
Net assets at beginning of year	XXX,XXX
Net assets at end of year	$XXX,XXX

[*The following paragraph is excerpted from Appendix B, "Basis for Conclusions," of FASB Statement No. 117.*]

114. The Board concluded that there is no compelling reason to prescribe the display of another measure similar to but not identical to a measure of change in unrestricted net assets. The Board observes that generally accepted accounting principles and the application of paragraph 7 of this Statement require display of an appropriately labeled subtotal for change in a class of net assets before the effects of an extraordinary item, the discontinuance of an operating segment, or an accounting change. For example, using the columnar Format B in Appendix C, a statement of activities would report the effects of an extraordinary item as follows:

	Unrestricted	Temporarily Restricted	Permanently Restricted	Total
Change in net assets before extraordinary items	$11,558	$(1,128)	$5,020	$15,450
Extraordinary items (Note X)	XXX	XXX	XXX	XXX
Change in net assets	$xx,xxx	$(x,xxx)	$x,xxx	$xx,xxx

Because generally accepted accounting principles require that these captions be modified appropriately when an organization reports the cumulative effect of an accounting change or the effects of disposal of a segment of its operations that may affect any one or more classes of its net assets, there is no need for this Statement to require the use of a specific label for the unrestricted or any one class of net assets. That would impose a standard more stringent than those that exist for business enterprises. The results of the Board's field test revealed that about half of the participants chose to report an intermediate measure of operations; however, they differed significantly in how they defined and described that measure. In its redeliberations of the Exposure Draft, the Board decided to add the disclosure and reporting requirements of paragraph 23 of this Statement.

APPENDIX B: Excerpt From FASB Statement of Financial Accounting Standards No. 116, *Accounting for Contributions Received and Contributions Made*[1]

[*Paragraph 141 of Appendix B, "Basis for Conclusions," of FASB Statement No. 116 is reprinted below.*]

141. The Board decided that certain transactions involving collection items should be reported separately from items of revenues, gains, expenses, and losses to reduce confusion resulting from the anomalies that result from not capitalizing collection items. The following illustrates one possible format[13] that may be used to satisfy the financial disclosure provisions of this Statement.

Organization M
Statement of Activities
For the Year Ended June 30, 19XX

	Unrestricted	Temporarily Restricted	Permanently Restricted	Total
Revenues and other support	XXX	XXX	XXX	XXX
Gain on sale of art that is not held in a collection	1			1
Net assets released from restrictions	XXX	(XXX)		
Total revenues, gains, and other support	XXX	XX	XXX	XXX
Expenses	XXX			XXX
Change in net assets before changes related to collection items not capitalized	XX	XX	XXX	XXX
Change in net assets related to collection items not capitalized:				
Proceeds from sale of collection items	5		10	15
Proceeds from insurance recoveries on destroyed collection items			1	1
Collection items purchased but not capitalized	—	—	(25)	(25)
	5	—	(14)	(9)
Change in net assets	XX	XX	XXX	XXX

---

[13] Appendix C of Statement 117 contains illustrations of several formats of statements of activities that might be adapted to comply with the provisions of this Statement.

---

[1] FASB Statement No. 116, *Accounting for Contributions Received and Contributions Made*, is copyrighted by the Financial Accounting Standards Board, 401 Merritt 7, P.O. Box 5116, Norwalk, Connecticut 06856-5116 U.S.A. This portion is reprinted with permission. Complete copies of this document are available from the FASB.

APPENDIX C: Excerpts From AICPA Audit and Accounting Guide *Not-for-Profit Organizations*

EXCERPT FROM CHAPTER 3, "BASIC FINANCIAL STATEMENTS"

[*Paragraph 3.21 is reprinted below.*]

3.21 An example of a note to the financial statements[10] that describes the nature of the prior-period(s) information would be as follows:

> The financial statements include certain prior-year summarized comparative information in total but not by net asset class. Such information does not include sufficient detail to constitute a presentation in conformity with generally accepted accounting principles. Accordingly, such information should be read in conjunction with the organization's financial statements for the year ended June 30, 20PY, from which the summarized information was derived.

---

[10] Because the note discusses information that does not pertain to the current-period financial statements, the note is not considered to be part of the current-period financial statements.

EXCERPT FROM CHAPTER 5, "CONTRIBUTIONS RECEIVED AND AGENCY TRANSACTIONS"

[*Paragraph 5.81 is reprinted below.*]

Illustrative Disclosures

5.81 The following section provides examples of notes to financial statements that illustrate some of the disclosures discussed in this chapter.

Example 1—Donor-Imposed Restrictions

Note X: Summary of Significant Accounting Policies

All contributions are considered to be available for unrestricted use unless specifically restricted by the donor. Amounts received that are designated for future periods or restricted by the donor for specific purposes are reported as temporarily restricted or permanently restricted support that increases those net asset classes. However, if a restriction is fulfilled in the same time period in which the contribution is received, the organization reports the support as unrestricted.

Example 2—Promises to Give

Note X: Summary of Significant Accounting Policies

Unconditional promises to give that are expected to be collected within one year are recorded at net realizable value. Unconditional promises to give that are expected to be collected in future years are recorded at the present value of their estimated future cash flows. The discounts on those amounts are computed using risk-free interest rates applicable to the years in which the promises are received. Amortization of the discounts is included in contribution revenue. Conditional promises to give are not included as support until the conditions are substantially met.

Note Y: Promises to Give

Included in "Contributions Receivable" are the following unconditional promises to give:

	20X1	20X0
Capital campaign	$1,220	
Restricted to future periods	795	$530
Unconditional promises to give before unamortized discount and allowance for uncollectibles	2,015	530
Less: Unamortized discount	(180)	(24)
Subtotal	1,835	506
Less: Allowance for uncollectibles	(150)	(30)
Net unconditional promises to give	$1,685	$476
Amounts due in:		
Less than one year	$1,220	
One to five years	725	
More than five years	70	
Total	$2,015	

Discount rates ranged from 4 percent to 4.5 percent and from 3.5 percent to 4 percent for 20X1 and 20X0, respectively.

In 20X0, the organization received $650 for a capital campaign which must be returned if the organization does not receive $1,300 in donations to the capital campaign. The $650 received was recorded on the 20X0 statement of financial position as a refundable advance. In 20X1, the organization received $500 in cash donations and $865 in unconditional promises to give to this campaign. As a result, the $650 was recognized as temporarily restricted contributions in 20X1.

In addition, the organization received the following conditional promises to give that are not recognized as assets in the statements of financial position:

	20X1	20X0
Conditional promise to give upon the establishment of a library program	$ 100	$100
Conditional promise to give upon obtaining $2,500 in unconditional promises to give to the capital campaign	5,000	

[*The following disclosure is encouraged but not required.*]

The organization received an indication of an intention to give from an individual long-time donor. The anticipated gift is an extensive collection of pre-Columbian textiles with great historical and artistic significance. The value of this intended gift has not been established, nor has the gift been recognized as an asset or contribution revenue.

Example 3—Accounting Policy for Contributed Property and Equipment

Note X: Summary of Significant Accounting Policies

Contributed property and equipment is recorded at fair value at the date of donation. In the absence of donor stipulations regarding how long the contributed assets must be used, the organization has adopted a policy of implying a time restriction on contributions of such assets that expires over the assets' useful lives. As a result, all contributions of property and equipment, and of assets contributed to acquire property and equipment, are recorded as restricted support.

OR

Contributed property and equipment is recorded at fair value at the date of donation. If donors stipulate how long the assets must be used, the contributions are recorded as restricted support. In the absence of such stipulations, contributions of property and equipment are recorded as unrestricted support.

Example 4—Contributed Services

The organization recognizes contribution revenue for certain services received at the fair value of those services. Those services include the following items:

	20X1	20X0
Home outreach program:		
Salaries:		
Social work interns—261 and 315 hours at $12.00 per hour	$ 3,132	$ 3,780
Registered nurse—200 and 220 hours at $15.00 per hour	3,000	3,300
Total salaries	6,132	7,080
Management and general:		
Accounting services	10,000	19,000
Total contributed services	$16,132	$26,080

In addition, approximately 80,000 hours, for which no value has been assigned, were volunteered by tutors in the home outreach program.

Example 5—Beneficial Interest in Assets Held by Others

In 19XX, the organization transferred $1,000,000 from its investment portfolio to the Any Town Community Foundation to establish an endowment fund. Under the terms of the agreement, in the first quarter of each year, the organization receives a distribution equal to the investment return generated by the transferred assets during the prior year. The organization can withdraw all or a portion of the original amount transferred, any appreciation on those transferred assets, or both, provided that a majority of the governing boards of the organization and the Foundation approve of the withdrawal. At the time of the transfer, the organization granted variance power to the Foundation. That power gives the Foundation the right to distribute the investment income to another not-for-profit organization of its choice if the organization ceases to exist or if the governing board of Any Town Community Foundation votes that support of the organization (*a*) is no longer necessary or (*b*) is inconsistent with the needs of the Any Town community. At June 30, 20X1, the endowment fund has a value of $1,234,567, which is reported in the statement of financial position as beneficial interest in assets held by others. (See paragraph 53 of FASB Statement No. 136.)

EXCERPT FROM CHAPTER 7, "OTHER ASSETS"

[*Paragraph 7.14 is reprinted below.*]

Illustrative Disclosures

7.14 This section provides examples of notes to the financial statements that illustrate some of the financial statement disclosures concerning collection items.

Example 1—Organizations That Capitalized Collections Prior to FASB Statement No. 116

Note X: Summary of Significant Accounting Policies

The organization has capitalized its collections since its inception. If purchased, items accessioned into the collection are capitalized at cost, and if donated, they are capitalized at their appraised or fair value on the accession date (the date on which the item is accepted by the Acquisitions Committee of the Board of Trustees). Gains or losses on the deaccession of collection items are classified on the statement of activities as unrestricted or temporarily restricted support depending on donor restrictions, if any, placed on the item at the time of accession.

Example 2—Organizations That Capitalize Collections Retroactively Upon Initial Adoption of FASB Statement No. 116

Note X: Summary of Significant Accounting Policies

In 20X1, the organization capitalized its collections retroactively in conformity with FASB Statement No. 116. To the extent that reliable records were available, the organization capitalized collection items acquired prior to 20X1 at their cost at the date of purchase or, if the items were contributed, at their fair or appraised value at the accession date (the date on which the item was accepted by the Acquisitions Committee of the Board of Trustees). Other collection items, particularly those acquired prior to 20X1 when detailed curatorial records began to be maintained, have been capitalized at their appraised or estimated current market value. In some cases, collection items held solely for their potential educational value or historical significance were determined to have no alternative use and were not assigned values for the purpose of capitalization. The collection items capitalized retroactively were determined to have a total value of $11,138,100. This amount is reflected as a change in accounting principle on the statement of activities.

Example 3—Organizations That Capitalize Their Collections Prospectively Upon Initial Adoption of FASB Statement No. 116

Note X: Summary of Significant Accounting Policies

Collection items acquired on or after July 1, 20X0: Accessions of these collection items are capitalized at cost, if the items were purchased, or at their appraised or fair value on the accession date (the date on which the item is accepted by the Acquisitions Committee of the Board of Trustees), if the items were contributed. Gains or losses from deaccessions of these items are reflected on the statement of activities as changes in the appropriate net asset classes, depending on the existence and type of donor-imposed restrictions.

Collection items acquired prior to July 1, 20X0: Collection items accessioned prior to July 1, 20X0 were recorded as decreases in unrestricted net assets, if the items were purchased. No financial statement recognition was made for contributed collection items. Proceeds from insurance recoveries or deaccessions of these items are reflected on the statements of activities as changes in the appropriate net asset classes, depending on the existence and type of donor-imposed restrictions.

Note Y: Accounting Change

In 20X1, the organization adopted FASB Statement No. 116. The organization has determined that the cost to capitalize its collections retroactively would be excessive because records of the cost of purchased items and of the fair value at the date of contribution of donated items are unreliable or do not exist. However, such information is available for current-year acquisitions and will be maintained on an ongoing basis. Therefore, the organization has elected to capitalize prospectively all collection items acquired after July 1, 20X0, the date of initial adoption of FASB Statement No. 116.

Note Z: Collections

The organization's collections are made up of artifacts of historical significance, scientific specimens, and art objects. Each of the items is cataloged for educational, research, scientific, and curatorial purposes, and activities verifying their existence and assessing their condition are performed continuously.

During 20X1, a significant number of American pioneer artifacts from the 1800s were destroyed while in transit to an exhibition in which they were to be displayed. Because those items were purchased prior to July 1, 20X0, the insurance proceeds of $22,000, which reimbursed the organization in full for the artifacts' fair value, are reflected as an increase in unrestricted net assets on the statement of activities. No other collection items were deaccessioned in 20X1 or 20X0.

Example 4—Organizations That Do Not Capitalize Collections

Note X: Summary of Significant Accounting Policies

The collections, which were acquired through purchases and contributions since the organization's inception, are not recognized as assets on the statement of financial position. Purchases of collection items are recorded as decreases in unrestricted net assets in the year in which the items are acquired, or as temporarily or permanently restricted net assets if the assets used to purchase the items are restricted by donors. Contributed collection items are not reflected on the financial statements. Proceeds from deaccessions or insurance recoveries are reflected as increases in the appropriate net asset classes.

Note Z: Collections

The organization's collections are made up of artifacts of historical significance, scientific specimens, and art objects that are held for educational, research, scientific, and curatorial purposes. Each of the items is cataloged, preserved, and cared for, and activities verifying their existence and assessing their condition are performed continuously. The collections are subject to a policy that requires proceeds from their sales to be used to acquire other items for collections.

During 20X1, a significant number of American pioneer artifacts from the 1800s were destroyed while in transit to an exhibition in which they were to be displayed. These artifacts were contributed in 20XX, with a restriction that limited any future proceeds from deaccessions to acquisitions of artifacts from a similar period. As a result, the insurance proceeds of $22,000, which reimbursed the organization in full for the artifacts' fair value, are reflected as an increase in temporarily restricted net assets on the statement of activities. No other collection items were deaccessioned in 20X1 or 20X0.

EXCERPTS FROM CHAPTER 13, "EXPENSES, GAINS AND LOSSES"

[Paragraphs 13.24 and 13.64 are reprinted below.]

13.24 Some ways in which the organization could display the results of the special event as part of its statement of activities are illustrated as follows:

Illustration 1

Changes in unrestricted net assets:		
Contributions		$200
Special event revenue	100	
Less: Costs of direct benefits to donors	(25)	
Net revenues from special events		75
Contributions and net revenues from special events		275
Other expenses:		
Program		60
Management and general		25
Fund raising		30
Total other expenses		115
Increase in unrestricted net assets		$160

Illustration 2

Changes in unrestricted net assets:		
Revenues:		
Contributions	$200	
Special event revenue	100	
Total revenues		300
Expenses:		
Program	60	
Costs of direct benefits to donors	25	
Management and general	25	
Fund raising	30	
Total other expenses		140
Increase in unrestricted net assets	$160	

Illustration 3

Changes in unrestricted net assets:		
Contributions		$270
Dinner sales	30	
Less: Costs of direct benefits to donors	(25)	
Gross profit on special events		5
Contributions and net revenues from special events		275

(continued)

Other expenses:	
Program	60
Management and general	25
Fund raising	30
Total other expenses	115
Increase in unrestricted net assets	$160

13.64—APPENDIX D: ILLUSTRATIONS OF DISCLOSURES

1. The disclosures discussed in paragraphs 13.53 and 13.54 are illustrated below. Alternative 1 reports the required and encouraged information in narrative format. Alternative 2 reports that information in tabular format, as well as information concerning joint costs incurred for each kind of activity by functional classification, which is neither required nor encouraged, but which is not prohibited.

Alternative 1

Note X. Allocation of Joint Costs

In 20XX, the organization conducted activities that included requests for contributions, as well as program and management and general components. Those activities included direct mail campaigns, special events, and a telethon. The costs of conducting those activities included a total of $310,000 of joint costs, which are not specifically attributable to particular components of the activities (joint costs). [*Note to reader: The following sentence is encouraged but not required.*] Joint costs for each kind of activity were $50,000, $150,000, and $110,000 respectively. These joint costs were allocated as follows:

Fund raising	$180,000
Program A	80,000
Program B	40,000
Management and general	10,000
Total	$310,000

Alternative 2

Note X. Allocation of Joint Costs

In 20XX, the organization conducted activities that included appeals for contributions and incurred joint costs of $310,000. These activities included direct mail campaigns, special events, and a telethon. Joint costs were allocated as follows:

	Direct Mail	Special Events	Telethon	Total
Fund raising	$40,000	$ 50,000	$ 90,000	$180,000
Program A	10,000	65,000	5,000	80,000
Program B		25,000	15,000	40,000
Management and general		10,000		10,000
Total	$50,000	$150,000	$110,000	$310,000

[***Note to reader:*** *Shading is used to highlight information that is neither required nor encouraged, but which is not prohibited. However, entities may prefer to disclose it. Disclosing the total joint costs for each kind of activity ($50,000, $150,000, and $110,000) is encouraged but not required.*]

APPENDIX D: Excerpt From FASB Statement of Financial Accounting Standards No. 136, *Transfers of Assets to a Not-for-Profit Organization or Charitable Trust That Raises or Holds Contributions for Others*

[Paragraph 109 of FASB Statement No. 136 is reprinted below.]

109. To the extent that an organization's activities include raising and distributing cash, the total amounts raised and distributed may be evident from a statement of cash flows prepared using the direct method for reporting operating cash flows. In addition, generally accepted accounting principles do not preclude entities from providing supplementary information or additional disclosures. An organization may provide a schedule reflecting fundraising efforts or campaign accomplishments or may disclose total amounts raised on the statement of activities, provided that amounts raised in an agent, trustee, or intermediary capacity are not shown as revenues. The following illustration provides three possible methods of displaying fundraising efforts in the revenue section of the statement of activities. Methods 2 and 3 display the total amounts raised.

An organization raises $6,000 of contributions, $100 of other support, and $4,000 accounted for as agent, trustee, or intermediary transactions because donors have specified beneficiaries without granting variance power. Of the $4,000 accounted for as agent, trustee, or intermediary transactions, the organization pays out $3,600 to specified beneficiaries and retains $400 as its administrative fee.

Method 1

Contributions	$6,000
Other support	100
Total support	6,100
Administrative fees retained on amounts designated by donors for specific organizations	400
Total support and revenue	$6,500

Method 2

Contributions	$6,000
Other support	100
Total support	6,100

(continued)

Other revenue:

Amounts designated by donors for specific organizations	$4,000	
Less: Amounts held for or remitted to those organizations	3,600	
Administrative fees retained on amounts designated by donors for specific organizations		400
Total support and revenue		$6,500

Method 3

Total amounts raised*	$10,000
Less: Amounts designated by donors for specific organizations	4,000
Total contributions	6,000
Other revenue:	
Other support	100
Administrative fees retained on amounts designated by donors for specific organizations	400
Total support and revenue	$ 6,500

The Board concluded that each of the methods reports the recipient organization's revenues ($6,500) in a way that is both easily understood by users of the financial statements and representationally faithful.

---

* Other terms, such as *campaign results* or *results of campaign efforts*, may be used.

APPENDIX E: Excerpt From FASB Statement of Financial Accounting Standards No. 124, *Accounting for Certain Investments Held by Not-for-Profit Organizations*

[*Paragraphs 103 through 106 from Appendix C, "Illustrative Examples," of FASB Statement No. 124 are reprinted below.*]

APPENDIX C: ILLUSTRATIVE EXAMPLES

Example of an Organization That Separates Investment Return Into Operating and Nonoperating Amounts

103. A statement of activities of Not-for-Profit Organization is illustrated below. Not-for-Profit Organization invests cash in excess of daily requirements in short-term investments; during the year, those investments earned $1,275. Most long-term investments of Not-for-Profit Organization's endowments are held in an investment pool, which earned income of $11,270 and had net gains of $15,450. Certain endowments are separately invested because of donors' requirements. The investments of those endowments earned income of $1,000 and increased in value by $1,500. One donor required that the net gains be added to the original endowment gift; that endowment's investment in the pool increased in value by $180.

Not-for-Profit Organization
Statement of Activities
Year Ended June 30, 19X1

	Unrestricted	Temporarily Restricted	Permanently Restricted	Total
Operating revenues, gains, and other support:				
Contributions	$ x,xxx	$ x,xxx		$xx,xxx
Fees	x,xxx			x,xxx
Investment return designated for current operations	11,025	4,500		15,525
Other	xxx			xxx
Net assets released from restrictions	xx,xxx	(xx,xxx)		
Total operating revenues, gains, and other support	xx,xxx	(x,xxx)		xx,xxx

(continued)

	Unrestricted	Temporarily Restricted	Permanently Restricted	Total
Operating expenses and losses:				
Program A	xx,xxx			xx,xxx
Program B	x,xxx			x,xxx
Program C	x,xxx			x,xxx
Management and general	x,xxx			x,xxx
Fund raising	x,xxx			x,xxx
Total operating expenses	xx,xxx			xx,xxx
Change in net assets from operations	x,xxx	(x,xxx)		x,xxx
Other changes:				
Investment return in excess of amounts designated for current operations	10,992	3,798	$ 180	14,970
[*Other items considered to be nonoperating*]	x,xxx	x,xxx		x,xxx
	xxx	xxx	xxx	xxx
Change in net assets	$xx,xxx	$ x,xxx	$ xxx	$xx,xxx

104. Not-for-Profit Organization would add the following illustrative text to its note to the financial statements that describes the measure of operations:

The board of trustees designates only a portion of the Organization's cumulative investment return for support of current operations; the remainder is retained to support operations of future years and to offset potential market declines. The amount computed under the endowment spending policy of the investment pool and all investment income earned by investing cash in excess of daily requirements are used to support current operations.

105. The following illustrative text and schedule would be added to a note to the financial statements about investments to provide the information about the composition of return and the reconciliation of investment return required by paragraph 14:

State law allows the board to appropriate so much of the net appreciation as is prudent considering the Organization's long- and short-term needs, present and anticipated financial requirements, expected total return on its investments, price level trends, and general economic conditions. Under the Organization's endowment spending policy, 5 percent of the average of the fair value at the end of the previous 3 years is appropriated to support current operations. The following schedule summarizes the investment return and its classification in the statement of activities:

	Unrestricted	Temporarily Restricted	Permanently Restricted	Total
Dividends, interest, and rents (net of expenses of $565)	$ 8,400	$ 3,870		$ 12,270
Net realized and unrealized gains	12,342	4,428	$180	16,950
Return on long-term investments	20,742	8,298	180	29,220
Interest on short-term investments	1,275			1,275
Total return on investments	22,017	8,298	180	30,495
Investment return designated for current operations	(11,025)	(4,500)		(15,525)
Investment return in excess of amounts designated for current operations	$ 10,992	$ 3,798	$180	$ 14,970

106. Often, as in the example above, the amount of investment return designated for current operations is less than the total return on investments for the year. An organization may be able to designate an amount for the support of operations even if the total investment return for the year is less than the amount computed under a spending-rate policy; for example, when the organization designates part of its cumulative investment return from prior years to support its current operations. In that case, the operating and nonoperating amounts should be labeled to faithfully represent their natures. For example, the amount excluded from operations, which is negative, might be labeled "Investment return reduced by the portion of cumulative net appreciation designated for current operations."

ABOUT THE AUTHORS

Richard F. Larkin, CPA, MBA (Harvard Business School), is technical director of not-for-profit accounting and auditing for BDO Seidman, LLP, in Bethesda, Maryland. He was previously a technical director of the Not-for-Profit Industry Services Group in the national office of PricewaterhouseCoopers LLP. He is a certified public accountant with 35 years of experience serving a wide variety of not-for-profit organizations as independent accountant, board member, treasurer, and consultant.

Mr. Larkin speaks and writes extensively on not-for-profit industry matters and is active in many professional and industry organizations. Professional memberships have included the Financial Accounting Standards Board Not-for-Profit Advisory Task Force, the AICPA Not-for-Profit Organizations Committee (two terms), the Evangelical Joint Accounting Committee, and the AICPA Not-for-Profit Audit Guide Task Force (chair). He has been a member of the governing boards of several not-for-profit organizations, and a member of the Board of Trustees of the Washington Cathedral Choral Society, and chair of its Finance Committee (also a singing member of the chorus).

Mr. Larkin is a co-author of the fifth edition of *Financial and Accounting Guide for Not-for-Profit Organizations* and the chapter on not-for-profit organizations in *The Accountants' Handbook,* as well as numerous articles. As a member of the Peace Corps, he taught business administration for two years at Haile Sellassie I University in Addis Ababa, Ethiopia.

Allen L. Fetterman, CPA, retired in 2003 from Loeb & Troper, where he spent 36 years serving not-for-profit organizations as an auditor and consultant, the last 25 years as a partner. In addition to his client responsibilities, he was the partner in charge of the firm's quality controls and technical resources, which included final review of all audit and attest reports, development of audit procedures and quality controls, issuance of technical releases to partners and staff, and coordination of the firm's continuing professional education program. He also lectured extensively on professional and technical issues to partners and staff.

Mr. Fetterman was a member of the AICPA's Not-for-Profit Organizations Committee and Not-for-Profit Guide Task Force. He has chaired the New York State Society of CPAs Professional Ethics and Audit Committees and is the current chair of the Not-for-Profit Organizations Committee. He has also served as vice-president of the New York State Society of CPAs. He currently sits as a judge on the AICPA Joint Trial Board.

Mr. Fetterman was an assistant professor of accounting at a local college and has lectured at Yale University and New York University. In addition, he is a member of the Faculty Bank of the Foundation for Accounting Education (FAE). He currently lectures throughout the country on not-for-profit accounting and auditing, federal compliance audits (OMB A-133), and tax compliance issues. He is a past recipient of both the AICPA's and the FAE's Outstanding Discussion Leader Award. He has written articles published in national accounting periodicals in the United States and Israel on accounting and taxes for not-for-profit organizations.

Mr. Fetterman received his BBA in Accounting from the City College of New York in 1968 and his MBA in Accounting from the Bernard M. Baruch College in 1972. He was elected to Beta Gamma Sigma, the national honorary society in business. He received his CPA certificate in 1973 and is a member of the AICPA and the New York State Society of CPAs.

Mr. Fetterman can be reached at allenfetterman@yahoo.com, or (845) 638-1460.